VEGETARIAN
PACIFIC NORTHWEST

A Guide to
Restaurants and Shopping

Vegetarians of Washington

HEALTHY LIVING PUBLICATIONS
Summertown , Tennessee

© 2008 Vegetarians of Washington

Executive Editors:	Amanda Strombom
	Stewart Rose
Managing Editor:	Griggs Irving
Editor:	Michael Angulo
Cover and Interior Design:	Cole Hornaday

Healthy Living Publications
A division of Book Publishing Company
PO Box 99
Summertown, TN 38483
1-888-260-8458
www.bookpubco.com

Printed on recycled paper in Canada
Published by Healthy Living Publications

ISBN 978-1-57067-211-8

12 11 10 09 08   1 2 3 4 5 6 7

The material in this book is not a substitute for professional medical care. Please consult your physician before making any changes to your diet, lifestyle, or medication.

Book Publishing Company is a member of Green Press Initiative. We chose to print this title on paper with postconsumer recycled content, processed without chlorine, which saved the following natural resources:

809 pounds of solid waste
6,300 gallons of water
1,1518 pounds of gases
17 trees
12 million BTU of energy

For more information, visit www.greenpressinitiative.org. Savings calculations thanks to the Environmental Defense Paper Calculator, www.papercalculator.org.

Library of Congress Cataloging-in-Publication Data

Vegetarian Pacific Northwest : a guide to restaurants and shopping / Vegetarians of Washington.

        p. cm.
    Includes index.
    ISBN 978-1-57067-211-8
    1. Vegetarian restaurants—Pacific, Northwest—
    Guidebooks. 2. Farmers' markets—Pacific,
    Northwest—Guidebooks. 3. Vegetarian cookery. I.
    Vegetarians of Washington.
      TX907.3.P323V45 2008
      641.5'636--dc22
                2008003261

Table of Contents

Acknowledgements

This book would not have been possible without the hard work and dedication of the members of the book team; Amanda Strombom, Stewart Rose, Griggs Irving, and Michael Angulo. Cole Hornaday did a splendid job in laying out the book and designing the cover and maps "thank you, Cole." One could not hope for a better publisher than the Book Publishing Company. Thanks to Bob and Cynthia Holzapfel and their team for all their support.

Thanks to the many restaurant reviewers who enabled us to broaden the reach of this book, especially Jessica Dadds, Casey McDonald, Susan Rose, and Theresa Bush, and to the team of Bastyr students, Laura Bady, Stephanie Bainton, Anne Buzzelli, Kathryn Hearn, Julie Starkel, and Garalynne Stiles-Smith who helped with fact checking. Thanks also to the many volunteers who helped create our first guidebook Veg-Feasting in the Pacific Northwest, on which much of the information in this book was based.

Definitions

In this book, we have used four terms to categorize the restaurants according to how friendly they are for vegetarians. While every restaurant is different, and so no categorization is perfect, the general guidelines to our reviewers were as follows:

Vegan: No items on the menu use any animal products at all.

Vegetarian: No items on the menu use meat, fish or poultry. Some menu items may be vegan, others may include dairy and/or eggs.

VeryVegFriendly: At least 50% of the menu is vegetarian, or there is a separate vegetarian menu.

VegFriendly: At least 25% of the menu is vegetarian, or can easily be made vegetarian with a simple substitution of available ingredients.

Introduction

The Vegetarian Scene in the Pacific Northwest

The vegetarian scene in the Northwest provides a delicious variety as well as a fascinating history. Several segments of the community have combined over time to form a unique Northwest flavor that continues to nourish the growing vegetarian scene to this day. The local recipe combines elements of the health food folks, people working for animal welfare, a new breed of environmentalists, and many people of faith.

How is it that these different groups found common ground in a vegetarian diet? And how did it lead to the Pacific Northwest having the most dynamic and exciting veg-scene in the country? To answer these questions we must turn the clock all the way back to the 1700s.

Benjamin Franklin was one of America's first vegetarians and also is credited with introducing the soybean to the United States. Who thought then that Ben Franklin's humble soybean would some day be found in the Northwest's most posh restaurants and trendiest natural food stores? The late 1800s brought some drastic changes in the American diet. Under the mistaken notion that heavily refined food and lots of meat represented progress and prosperity, the national diet changed to include more of these foods. Enter white bread and refined sugar, and spoiled and decaying meat so bad that it sparked national scandals made famous by Upton Sinclair in *The Jungle.* Enter also an increase in diseases such as heart disease, stroke, cancer, diabetes, and several digestive disorders. Many people looked at the changes in our diet and health and wondered if it wasn't time to return to a healthier, more traditional diet.

About this time, one group in particular advocated a return to a healthier diet. In fact, it advocated a return all the way back to the diet of Adam and Eve. That group was the Seventh Day Adventists, a new church especially popular in the Northwest. This group worked to improve the diet and health of every man, woman, and child in the Northwest and throughout the country, by actively promoting a healthy vegetarian diet and by founding new health food companies. These companies also manufactured some of the early meat substitutes that have recently become so popular.

By the early 1900s some other church groups began recommending a vegetarian diet. For example, the Unity Christian church and the Salvation Army started to promote a vegetarian diet at about this time. A short time later many people in other Christian denominations and also many Jews began to adopt a vegetarian diet from a position of faith. The vegetarian movement in the Northwest and in the rest of the country was now gaining momentum.

By the time the Roaring Twenties arrived, modern medicine was coming into its own with major advances in medication and surgery to benefit both young and old. But doctors also began noticing an increase in the incidence of those diseases they suspected were linked to the national changes in diet. They noticed that vegetarians were usually the healthiest folks in town. The day would come when everyone from country doctors to the most advanced medical researchers would tout the benefits of a vegetarian diet. Health conscious people across the Northwest would start saying "please pass the tofu" and natural food markets would spring up across the region to meet the demand.

As the country grew so did the need for large quantities of inexpensive food. Old MacDonald's farm was a thing of the past. Enter the factory farm and really hard times for the animals. Animal welfare groups emerged all over the country, including in the Northwest. These folks, motivated by humanitarian considerations, became enthusiastic proponents of a vegetarian diet, saving the animals with every bite.

Along with the many innovations of the 1960s came a new and vital influence in the vegetarian movement. At about this time, more and more people started to question the healthfulness of a high-meat diet, a diet also full of highly refined foods and artificial ingredients. There was a call to get back to a more natural diet in general and a vegetarian diet in particular. Many people were also getting down to business as the Northwest became home to a number of vegetarian food companies founded with a vegetarian vision. Soon natural food stores, co-ops, and vegetarian restaurants began springing up all over the Northwest. Bulk bins for grains, beans sold by the pound, and scrambled tofu for breakfast were becoming more common. Around this time, Yoga also was becoming popular in the Northwest, with many Yoga instructors advocating a vegetarian diet to their students.

During the 1970s and '80s the environmental movement came into its own. We heard about the Amazon and other rainforests being cut and burned down primarily to raise meat. The oil shortages of the 1970s made us more conscious of just how much more oil was needed to produce meat compared to vegetarian foods. We smelled the runoff from factory farms into our streams. Now we know that animal-based agriculture causes more global warming than all the cars, trains, planes, and ships in the world put together. Many environmentalists came to realize that following a vegetarian diet is a way to help preserve the environment for future generations.

The 1980s and '90s brought quite a bit of immigration to the Northwest, with a substantial number of new people coming from Asia. Many of these people were Buddhists from China, Thailand, and Vietnam, and they brought a tradition of vegetarianism with them. Others came from India, where following a vegetarian diet is an age-old Hindu tradition. The new wave of immigration led to a new wave of vegetarian restaurants featuring a rich variety of ethnic cuisine. A new health-conscious trend among some Mexican restaurants offered new menu items such as vegan burritos. The choice of vegetarian cuisine in the Northwest was growing quickly.

From fine dining in Seattle and Portland's vegetarian restaurants and bistros to great home cooking in Washington and Oregon's small town cafés and eateries, the Northwest now offers culinary delights to satisfy every taste and desire. Not to be overlooked is the monthly dining event of the Vegetarians of Washington. This culinary happening features a different restaurant, cookbook author or chef every month at a downtown Seattle location that draws people from near and far.

There's also Vegfest, the country's largest and most exciting vegetarian food festival. Vegfest features chefs from all over the country who show their magic and share their secrets in large-scale cooking demonstrations. Doctors and dietitians are on hand to talk about the latest health advantages of a vegetarian diet. Vegfest also features the largest vegetarian bookstore in the world. Here in the Northwest, we love to try new food. Vegfest satisfies this desire by featuring more than 600 different kinds of food to taste. Each year, this food sampling extravaganza serves the vegetarian and veg-curious public with more free samples of delicious food from every company you've ever heard of and a few you haven't, but soon will.

Following a vegetarian diet never has been more popular and has now started to go mainstream. Vegetarian food is all the rage and we invite you to discover the delicious vegetarian cuisine to be found in the Pacific Northwest.

Dining

Dining out is one of life's true pleasures, with restaurants specializing in different cuisines and offering unique atmospheres. As more people discover the many benefits of a vegetarian diet, there has been a steady increase in the number of vegetarian restaurants throughout the Pacific Northwest. It's also a growing trend for general restaurants to offer more vegetarian options.

Dining at a totally vegetarian restaurant is easy since you have a wide selection to choose from. You'll often find that most items on the menu can also be made without dairy or eggs if requested. Most of the vegetarian restaurants are used to receiving special requests, and many include dairy and egg alternatives on the menu.

Most Indian, Thai, Chinese, and Vietnamese restaurants have many tasty vegetarian options to choose from. However, other cuisines should not be overlooked. Often Ethiopian and Middle Eastern restaurants have good vegetarian choices on their menu. In fact, even if you skip looking at the menu and just ask for a Veggie Combination at any Ethiopian restaurant, you'll always be brought a platter covered in delicious vegetarian dishes. Bean burritos and enchiladas are good choices at Mexican restaurants, although they do tend to include a lot of cheese. Tip: ask for whole beans to avoid those cooked in lard.

Vegetarian food is also showing up in some surprising places. Many steak and seafood houses are now offering some rather tasty dishes to attract the vegetarian customer. At the very least, you can get a veggie burger in many American and fast-food restaurants these days and even a veggie dog at many baseball stadiums.

Using this guide to local restaurants, you will always have plenty of delicious choices available to you. On occasion, of course, you'll need to eat at a restaurant with few, if any, vegetarian options. If there's nothing you feel comfortable ordering on the menu, we recommend that you ask whether a special vegetarian meal could be prepared and specify what you would like, choosing ingredients you can see are available from the menu. Chefs are often happy to receive such special requests. Many is the time that the chef has come out to relate his delight at having the opportunity to be creative and prepare a vegetarian meal. The result can be a dish that is truly inspired.

There have never been so many dining options for vegetarians to choose from. We encourage you to look at finding tasty vegetarian options when dining out as an adventure. Enjoy!

Shopping

Shopping for the vegetarian kitchen is easy and fun. We are fortunate, here in the Northwest, to have a wide variety of choices. All you need is information about where to shop, which you'll find in this book, and ideas on what to buy and how to prepare it (see our cookbook, *The Veg-Feasting Cookbook*). There are three broad categories of stores offering vegetarian options: food co-ops, natural food stores, and mainstream supermarkets.

You may be surprised to learn that the Northwest has many food co-ops both large and small. The odds are excellent that there is one within easy driving distance from your home. Food co-ops sell their memberships to the public. By purchasing one you will become a part owner of the store, with voting rights that give you a say in how the co-op is run, if you wish. The food co-ops became involved in the natural food business very early on and so they have lots of experience. Often they have policies regarding quality and variety that make them an especially good place to shop. Many also offer educational programs to help you learn more about your food choices. Try one out. You don't need to be a member to shop there. However, if you do decide to join, you'll soon find that the co-op discounts are well worth the small joining fee.

Natural food stores, both large and small, abound in the Northwest. You'll find everything from small local mom-and-pop stores to larger supermarket style stores. The small stores offer well-chosen stock, and the staff can usually spend time offering advice and making special orders. These smaller stores know their clientele well and will usually have just what you're looking for. The larger natural food stores offer the advantage of a wide variety of items and convenience sections such as a deli, bakery, and cafeteria. They are also usually open with extended hours and feature many in-store demos so that you can sample some of the latest product lines.

Not to be overlooked are the mainstream supermarket chains. While they do not offer nearly the same level of choices, they are carrying an increasing amount of vegetarian options these days. In some of today's supermarkets, one can often find a couple of brands of soy milk and tofu, along with some other healthy products. Supermarkets are beginning to recognize that vegetarian food choices are becoming increasingly popular. Beyond specialty items, they also carry a good line of both fresh and frozen produce. Look to buy organic food whenever possible and affordable. Organic food has the advantage of being grown without pesticides and herbicides. You can often save money by buying organic produce that is in season and grown locally. Don't overlook the frozen produce. Picked at just the right time, freshness is well-preserved and just waiting to be cooked.

Start by getting to know your local co-op, natural food store or supermarket natural food section. Take a stroll up and down the aisles and see how many of the products there are familiar to you. Keep an eye out for new varieties and flavors of old favorites. When you come upon an unfamiliar item try to learn something about it. Be willing to experiment. Most stores will be happy to make a special order for you if you can't find what you want. Make shopping an adventure in good health!

From the Farm

In addition to retail stores, there are two special ways in which vegetarians and their friends can purchase fresh produce. Farmers' Markets and Community Supported Agriculture (CSA) offer consumers direct access to farm foods, and to the farmers who prune, plant, and harvest these foods. This contact has been recognized as mutually beneficial to both the growers and buyers, and it is being actively promoted on both the local and state levels.

For a thoroughly rewarding experience, go visit the next Farmers' Market in a town near you. These happen once a week (occasionally twice), usually on a parking lot or a closed-off street block. You'll find all the energy and bustle of a street fair, a scene as old as civilization, but it's actually a relatively new and growing trend throughout the USA. Farmers of all kinds, including orchardists, mushroom cultivators, and herb growers, take a day to come in from the countryside and group together to sell their produce. Almost always outside and under tents, people from the city get a first-hand look at the freshest organic fruits and vegetables possible. The mix changes weekly with the seasons. Early shoppers get the plumpest peaches, the brightest broccoli, and the most luscious lettuce. You can talk to the actual person (and often their spouse and kids) from whose soil these food crops were pulled or picked. Farmers' Markets give producer and purchaser a chance to meet, share and learn from each other.

Farms with Community Supported Agriculture (CSA) programs are often called Subscription Farms. CSA customers can contract yearly in advance with a nearby farm for the purchase (and often delivery) of fresh organic fruits and vegetables, with occasionally flowers and a handful of herbs added to the weekly boxes. In the deep of winter, "subscribers," who often number in the hundreds, invest a sum of money with the CSA farmer. This allows the farmer to buy seeds and equipment and hire personnel in order to grow the crops promised. Then, usually starting in June and continuing for approximately 25 weeks, the subscriber receives a box of fresh seasonal fruits and vegetables. Often friendly recipes and notes accompany the weekly box, helping subscribers understand how to cook and serve new and different vegetables and fruits. Most CSA farmers welcome farm visits and even have family events. Some CSA offer agricultural apprenticeships. A few CSAs offer full year 52-week subscriptions. CSA subscribers often develop a natural bonding with "their farm" and become involved more directly with the agricultural system.

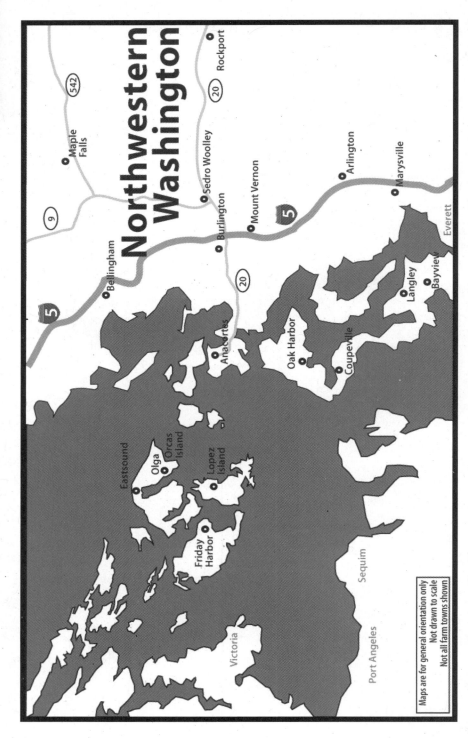

Northwestern Washington

Maps are for general orientation only
Not drawn to scale
Not all farm towns shown

Northwestern Washington

ANACORTES

Anacortes Health & Nutrition
1020 Seventh St • Anacortes • (360) 293-8849

Old-fashioned health and nutrition store on beautiful Fidalgo Island with fresh organic produce and healthy foods. Open Mon-Fri 9am-6pm, Sat-Sun 10am-6pm.

Anacortes Farmers' Market
Saturday, 9am-2pm, May-October
7th Street & R Avenue at the Depot Arts Center
www.anacortesfarmersmarket.org

ARLINGTON

Taco Del Mar
3707 172nd St NE • Arlington • (360) 653 8878 • www.tacodelmar.com
See review – Seattle

BAYVIEW

Bayview Farmers' Market
Saturday and Sunday, 10am-2pm, April-October
SR 525 and Bayview
www.bayviewfarmersmarket.com

BELLINGHAM

DINING

Casa Que Pasa
1415 Railroad Ave • Bellingham • (360) 756-8226

VeryVegFriendly • Mexican • Daily 11am-midnight • Entrées $5

Known for being inexpensive with huge proportions. Vegetarian dishes are clearly classified. Specialty burritos weigh in at one pound for under $5. About half the burritos on the menu are vegetarian, with some vegan options. Relaxed atmosphere full of music and color, with a friendly and accommodating staff.

The Lemon Grass Restaurant
111 N Samish Way • Bellingham • (360) 676-4102

VeryVegFriendly • Thai • Lunch & dinner • Full service & take out • Entrées $5-10

Alleged to be the best Thai food in town! The warm, exotic, inviting atmosphere is not to be missed. Excellent vegetarian and vegan choices on the menu, all including salad. Necessary accommodations will be made for vegan/vegetarian requests as the staff is familiar with these diets. There is usually no more than a 20-30 minute wait on weekends, and it is well worth it. Parking is free, which is rare for many restaurants in Bellingham

The Old Town Café
316 West Holly St • Bellingham • (360) 671-4431

VeryVegFriendly • Breakfast & lunch daily • Full service • Entrées $5-10

The Old Town Café has a traditional and cozy atmosphere. With a menu almost entirely made up of vegetarian meals, there are also some excellent vegan options. They serve an assortment of juices, espresso drinks, omelets, salads, and sandwiches made up of natural, local, and organic products. Delicious pastries made on-site. Avoid the hustle and bustle of everyday life and step into the slow-paced, relaxed environment of the Old Town Café.

Supon's Thai Cuisine
1213 Dupont St • Bellingham • (360) 734-6838

VeryVegFriendly • Thai • Daily lunch & dinner • Full service • Entrées $5-10

Located on the outskirts of Bellingham, Supon's Thai Cuisine is a casual restaurant with great service. Though the sauces aren't usually made vegetarian, they will be happy to remake the order. This is especially helpful if ordering Phad Thai or other common dishes with previously made sauces. The spring rolls are vegan and excellent. Good assortment of bottled juices and other drinks.

Swan Café (Community Food Co-op)
1220 N Forest • Bellingham • (360) 734-8158 • www.communityfood.coop

VeryVegFriendly • Eclectic deli • Items under $5

Located inside the Community Food Co-op, the Swan Café offers items from tofu cutlets and tempeh salads to vegan desserts such as fudge, cake, and other pastries. All items are clearly and accurately labeled if vegan or vegetarian. The espresso bar carries both soy and rice milk, and offers a variety of delicious smoothies that can be made vegan. Casual atmosphere and friendly service. Non-members charged 6.5% on all items, but if you're a member of another co-op, this should be honored.

Taco Del Mar
122 East Magnolia St • Bellingham • (360) 734-0313 • www.tacodelmar.com
4277 Meridian St • Bellingham • (360) 255-2254
See review – Seattle

SHOPPING

Bargainica
902 N State St • Bellingham • (360) 738-9888

Bellingham's discount organic and natural food store is located on State Street and also has its own shelves in the Terra Organica store at the Public Market. By taking advantage of manufacturer's deals and volume purchases, buying odd lots and cosmetically damaged products, every product offered is 20%-80% below retail price. A fun place to shop and the best place to save on quality food. Open daily 9am-9pm.

Community Food Co-op
1220 N Forest • Bellingham • (360) 734 8158 • www.communityfood.coop.com

The local premier full service, natural foods grocery store with Whatcom County's only certified organic produce department. Vegan and vegetarian items available across departments. A comfortable and relaxed atmosphere. The café area has nice sunny exposure. Planning to open a second store in North Bellingham, Summer 2009. Open daily 8am-9pm.

Terra Organica
1530 Cornwall Ave • Bellingham • (360) 715-8020

Located in the Bellingham Public Market, Terra Organica is the dream store for anyone who loves organic food. Over 99% of the products are organic or wild-crafted. All products are thoroughly researched to ensure they are ethically produced and the purest available. Every Sunday 25% off all produce. Mon-Fri 7am-10pm, Sat 8am-10pm, Sun 9am-10pm

Trader Joe's
2410 James Street • Bellingham • (360) 734-5166
See review – Seattle

FROM THE FARM

Bellingham Farmers' Markets
Wednesday, 3-7pm, June-September
Fairhaven Village Green behind Village Books

Saturday, 10am-3pm, April-December
Downtown at Railroad & Chestnut
www.bellinghamfarmers.org

BURLINGTON

Adventist Book Center

334 East Fairhaven Ave • Burlington • (360) 755-1032

Very popular with the vegetarian community. A large selection of vegetarian foods, including very wide choice of meat substitutes such as hot dogs, chicken, etc. Dried fruits, healthy snack foods, cereals, soy milks, soups, etc. are also available. Extensive selection of books on health and nutrition, and cookbooks. Hours are Tues, Thurs 12-6pm, Wed 3pm-6pm, Sun 12-4pm.

Taco Del Mar

1773 S Burlington Blvd • Burlington • (360) 757-8507 • www.tacodelmar.com
See review – Seattle

COUPEVILLE

Coupeville Farmers' Market

Saturday, 10am-2pm, April-October
Alexander and 8th Street

EASTSOUND

Orcas Island Farmers' Market

Saturday, 10am-3pm, May-October
Eastsound Village Green, just north of the Historical Museum
www.orcasislandfarmersmarket.org

Maple Rock Farm

845 Pinneo Road • Eastsound • (360) 376-6080 • www.maplerockfarm.com

Founded in 2000, Maple Rock Farm currently harvests four acres of diverse organic produce, including berries and fruit. The farm provides fresh, pesticide-free, locally grown produce to residents of Orcas Island and hosts special events throughout the year.

FRIDAY HARBOR

San Juan Farmers' Market

Saturday, 10am-1pm, April-October
2nd & Blair-Courthouse parking lot

LANGLEY

The Star Store & Star Store Basics
201 First St & 199 2nd St • Langley • (360) 221-5222
www.starstorewhidbey.com

A small, full-service supermarket committed to quality and customer service. Their store just across the street is stocked with supplements, homeopathy, health-and-beauty and non-food, earth-friendly products. Many meat alternatives, good frozen selection. Outstanding quality organic produce. Open Mon-Sat 8am-8pm, Sun 8am-7pm.

Tilth Farmers' Market
Saturday, 10am-2pm, May-October
Hwy 525 at Thompson Road
www.southwhidbeytilth.org

MAPLE FALLS

Mt. Baker Farmers' Market
Sunday, 10am-3pm, June-October
Mt. Baker Hwy
www.mtbakermarket.com

MARYSVILLE

Taco Del Mar
8825 34th Ave NE • Marysville • (360) 654-2960 • www.tacodelmar.com
See review – Seattle

MOUNT VERNON

DINING

The Deli Next Door
202 S 1st St • Mt Vernon • (360) 336-3886

VeryVegFriendly • Deli • Daily 8am-9pm (open 9am-8pm Sun)

Not really next door, but actually in the Skagit Valley Co-op, one of the friendliest, all-product natural food stores in this agricultural area. In addition to the expected soups and salads and lots of vegetarian items, The Deli has specials like Veggie Samosas and Falafal Nuggets. Take your eats upstairs to the mezzanine and relax watching the activities in the store floor below.

SHOPPING

Skagit Valley Co-op

202 S First St • Mt Vernon • (360) 336-9777

One of the friendliest, all-product natural food stores in this agricultural area. Highly community centered. Great in-store deli. Open Mon-Sat 8am-9pm, Sun 9am-8pm.

FROM THE FARM

Mount Vernon Farmers' Market

Wednesday, 2:30pm-5:30pm, June-September
Skagit Valley Hospital at 1415 E Kincaid

Saturday, 9am-1pm, May-October
The Revetment on the river at Gates & Main

OAK HARBOR

Amy's Garden

2814 N Torpedo Rd • Oak Harbor • (360) 240-8166

Amy's "earth-friendly farm" provides local families with fresh vegetables, fruit, and old-fashioned flowers. Year-round Community-Supported Agriculture program and produce delivery service serving Whidbey Island and Anacortes.

Oak Harbor Public Market

Thursday, 4pm-7pm, May-September
Hwy 20 next to Visitor Center

OLGA (ORCAS ISLAND)

Doe Bay Café

107 Doe Bay Road • Olga • (360) 376-8059 • www.doebay.com/cafe.html

VeryVegFriendly • Northwest • Summer daily breakfast, lunch and dinner • Winter weekends only

The Doe Bay Resort is a great place for a relaxing getaway, offering everything from fully fitted 3 bedroom cabins to yurts and camping sites. Doe Bay Café offers a varying menu of vegetarian and seafood options, depending on the season and availability. Menu choices are delicious and inventive using the freshest local ingredients. Phone ahead for the menu and to check opening hours.

SEDRO WOOLLEY

Sedro Woolley Farmers' Market
Wednesday, 3pm-7pm, May-October
Hammer Heritage Square (Ferry and Metcalf)

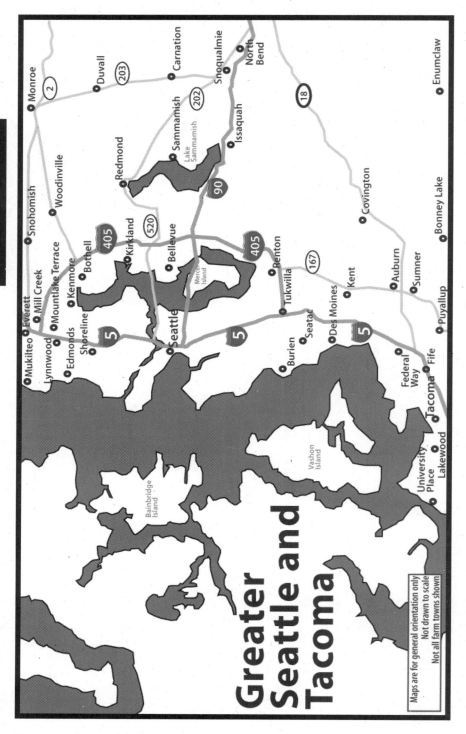

Greater Seattle and Tacoma

Maps are for general orientation only
Not drawn to scale
Not all farm towns shown

Greater Seattle and Tacoma

AUBURN

Adventist Book Center
5000 Auburn Way • Auburn • (253) 833-6707

Very popular with the vegetarian community. A large selection of vegetarian foods, including very wide choice of meat substitutes such as hot dogs, chicken, etc. Dried fruits, healthy snack foods, cereals, soy milks, soups, etc. are also available. Extensive selection of books on health and nutrition, and cookbooks. Open Mon-Thurs 9am-6pm, Fri 9am-3pm and Sun 10am-5pm.

Taco Del Mar
1202 Supermall Way #103 • Auburn • (253) 735-5089 • www.tacodelmar.com
1702 Auburn Way N • Auburn • (253) 351-8888
See review – Seattle

BELLEVUE

DINING

California Pizza Kitchen
595 106th Ave NE • Bellevue • (425) 454-2545 • www.cpk.com

VegFriendly • Pizza & pasta • Daily lunch & dinner • Entrées around $10

This popular, family-friendly pizza restaurant chain has a long list of pizza choices, with over a third being vegetarian. Choices include Vegetarian with Japanese Eggplant, Wild Mushroom or Southwestern Black Bean (Tostada) pizzas. There are also several pasta and focaccia sandwich options. If you're vegan, ask them to hold the cheese. Service is quick and efficient.

Chantanee
150 105th Ave NE • Bellevue • (425) 455-3226 • www.chantanee.com

VeryVegFriendly • Thai • Daily lunch & dinner • Full service & take out • Entrées $5-10

Because the owner is a vegetarian, that menu alone lists 40 items and the portions are very generous. It is reported that the spring rolls are wonderful and there are 12 on the plate. Coconut soup is superb and chock full of tofu and veggies. Phad Mee tofu is perfectly spiced and a hit. Best of all, the service is unbelievable. Fresh orchids on every table and a huge bouquet of them in the spotless (women's) restroom.

Chutneys

938 110th Ave NE • Bellevue • (425) 467-0867 • www.chutneys.com

VeryVegFriendly • Indian cuisine • Lunch (with buffet), dinner • Entrées $10-20

A large portion of the menu is vegetarian. The vegetable Pakoras are just perfect and their fire-roasted Eggplant Bharta has a wonderful smoky taste. Every dish sampled is delicious. The elegant décor is very tasteful and the convenient location a bonus. The Chutneys restaurant in Seattle has a similar reputation.

India Gate

3080 148th Ave SE (Eastgate) • Bellevue • (425) 747-1075

Very VegFriendly • Indian • Daily lunch & dinner • Sun dinner only • Entrées $5-10

Bellevue has so many wonderful Indian restaurants and this one does not disappoint. Dishes are perfectly executed and the portions are substantial. The Saag Paneer is creamy and is perfectly spiced. The Eggplant Bhartha is smoky with a hint of tomato. The Vegetable Samosas are the best around, especially with the coriander mint chutney on top. Don't forget the rich and dreamy rice pudding.

King and I Thai Cuisine

10509 Main St • Bellevue • (425) 462-9337 • www.howspicy.com/kingandi

VeryVegFriendly • Thai • Open daily • Entrées $5-10

From the extensive vegetarian menu Tom Ka Gai stands out (coconut broth with tofu and mushrooms) but the Phad See Ew is SUPERB! Its wide rice noodles and broccoli are perfectly spiced in a flavorful sauce. Both brown and white rice are offered. The décor is noticeably artistic.

Mayuri Indian Cuisine

15400 NE 20th St • Bellevue • (425) 641-4442 • www.mayuriseattle.com

VegFriendly • North & South Indian • Lunch & dinner • Full service or take out Entrées $5-10

A beautiful, friendly family restaurant where vegetarian, vegan and non-veg can be happy. Dinners are well-sized, and the Thali dinners are enormous. The staff is warm and willing to help make changes and suggestions for vegan diners. There is often live entertainment, noted on their website. The restaurant is associated with Mayuri Grocery in Redmond. The owner is a devoted vegetarian. A local favorite.

Mediterranean Kitchen

103 NE Bellevue Way • Bellevue • (425) 462-9422
www.mediterraneankitchens.net

VegFriendly • Middle Eastern • Daily lunch & dinner, Sunday dinner only • Full service, take out and catering • Entrées $10-20

People stand outside shivering in the winter to be able to enjoy this restaurant which has seven vegetarian main dishes and virtually all vegetarian appetizers. Portions are gargantuan and service is attentive and friendly. The enormous Meze platter overflows with 6 delicious appetizers which could make a filling dinner for three hungry adults. Baskets of pita bread keep coming and the various soups are always vegetarian and hearty with loads of flavor. The homemade Baklava is delicate and light.

Moghul Palace

10303 NE 10th St • Bellevue • (425) 451-1909

VegFriendly • Indian• Luncheon buffet Mon-Sat • Dinner daily • Entrées $5-10

This restaurant offers a selection of vegetarian entrées that are made with organic spices and can be ordered as mild, medium, hot or extra hot. A variety of breads are cooked in a charcoal clay oven.

Nature's Pantry Juice Bar

10200 NE 10th St • Bellevue • (425) 454-0170

VegFriendly • Juice, Salads & Deli • Open Daily all day • Entrées less than $5

For a quick healthy meal, you can't beat Natures Pantry Juice Bar. There is a large selection of fresh organic juices and smoothies, where you can add special ingredients such as spirulina or wheat germ. Choose from salads, wraps, noodle dishes, and sandwiches for a light lunch or quick evening meal. Seating is mostly at the bar.

Square Lotus

3540A Factoria Blvd SE • Bellevue • (425) 679-0680

VeryVegFriendly • Vietnamese • Daily lunch & dinner • Entrees $7-$10

On the corner of Loehmann's Plaza in Factoria, this elegant restaurant features a full vegetarian menu alongside its meat-based Vietnamese menu. Favorite dishes include Mango Chicken, Lemongrass Tuna Fish and Beef Cashew, all made with faux meat. Most dishes are vegan; just a few include egg noodles. Service is quick and discrete. Everything is beautifully presented, often on square plates giving rise to the restaurant's name.

Taco Del Mar

575 Bellevue Square 1008 • Bellevue • (425) 450-0094 • www.tacodelmar.com
677 120th Ave SE • Bellevue • (425) 646-9041
See review – Seattle

Thai Chef
1645 140th Ave NE • Bellevue • (425) 562-7955

VegFriendly • Thai • Daily lunch & dinner • Entrées $5-10

The entrées are sure to please both vegetarian and non-vegetarian fans of Thai food. Great appetizers. Family friendly.

The Thai Kitchen
14116 NE 20th St • Bellevue • (425) 641-9166

VeryVegFriendly • Thai • Daily lunch & dinner • Full service & take out • Entrées $5-10

The vegetarian menu has soup, appetizers and a few select entrées. The meals are served as spicy as you want and are flavorful. Friendly courteous staff provides fast service.

Udupi Palace
15600 NE 8th St • Bellevue • (425) 649-0355

Vegetarian • Indian • Daily lunch & dinner • Full service • Entrées $5-10

Nestled between a doll store and a bakery at one end of Crossroads Mall, Udupi Palace is a truly authentic Indian vegetarian experience. With clean simple décor, and all Indian dishes, such as Cashew Pongal and Masala Dosa, this restaurant is especially popular with the local Indian population.

World Wrapps
228 Bellevue Square Mall • Bellevue • (425) 635-0103 • www.worldwrapps.com

VegFriendly • International Fast Food • Lunch & dinner around $5 • Special menu for kids.

World Wrapps is a gift to vegetarians! It's incredibly flavorful, vegetarian fast food that's healthy too. There are five vegetarian sandwich wraps available—Bombay Curry Veggie, Tofu Mushroom Teriyaki, Bean & Cheese, Baja Veggie and Portobello Mushroom and Goat Cheese. Vegans, the cheese can be left out of most of the dishes. The smoothies are rich and fruity, with ingredients like blackberries and mangos. It's fast food, but tastes like it isn't.

Zen Yai Noodle House
15400 NE 20th St • Bellevue • (425) 378-1100

VegFriendly • Thai • Daily lunch & dinner • Full service or take-out • Entrée $5-10

Dining in this tranquil and upscale décor, you'll find many items on the menu available in vegetarian and vegan options. Favorites are several soup selections, the Vietnamese Hand Rolls and Eggplant with Basil. Several soup selections are vegetarian.

SHOPPING

Nature's Pantry
10201 NE 10th • Bellevue • (425) 454-0170

For 33 years, a family-run natural/organic store carrying fresh organic produce, bulk items, fresh juices, vitamin and body care lines. There is a deli with very reasonable prices in spite of a high-end appearance. Excellent customer service from knowledgeable employees. Open Mon-Fri 9am-7pm, Sat 9am-6pm, Sun 11am-5pm.

Trader Joe's
15400 NE 20th St • Bellevue • (425) 643-6885 • www.traderjoes.com
See description – Seattle

Uwajimaya
15555 NE 24th St • Bellevue • (425) 747-9012 • www.uwajimaya.com

A smaller version of the Seattle store, it is an excellent source for Asian specialties, spices, and vegetarian and vegan items. Gifts, household items, and cookware also available. Restaurant, bakery, and deli with some vegetarian and vegan items. Open daily 9am-10pm.

Whole Foods Market
888 116th Avenue NE • Bellevue • (425) 462-1400
See review – Seattle

FROM THE FARM

Bellevue Farmers' Markets
Tuesday, Noon-5pm, May-October
Crossroads Bellevue parking lot, 156th Ave NE & NE 8th
www.crossroadsbellevue.com

Thursday, 3pm-7pm, May-October
First Presbyterian Church parking lot, 1717 Bellevue Way NE
www.bellevuefarmersmarket.org

BONNEY LAKE

Taco Del Mar
21102 SE 410 E • Bonney Lake • Opening soon • www.tacodelmar.com
See review – Seattle

BOTHELL

DINING

Pen Thai Restaurant
10107 Main St • Bothell • (425) 398-7300 • www.penthai.com

VegFriendly • Lunch & dinner • Closed Sun

Like its sister restaurant, Chantanee in Bellevue, the vegetarian menu alone lists 40 items and the portions are very generous. It is reported that the spring rolls are wonderful and there are 12 on the plate. Coconut soup is superb and chock full of tofu and veggies. Phad Mee tofu is perfectly spiced and a hit. Best of all, the service is unbelievable.

Taco del Mar
22833 Bothell-Everett Hwy #151 • Bothell • (425) 481-0737
www.tacodelmar.com
See review – Seattle

FROM THE FARM

Bothell Farmers' Market at Country Village
Friday, 10am-3pm, May-September
238th & Bothell-Everett Hwy (SR 527)

BURIEN

DINING

Taco Del Mar
116 SW 148th St • Burien • (206) 243-4675 • www.tacodelmar.com
See review – Seattle

SHOPPING

The Grainery
13629 1st Ave S • Burien • (206) 244-5015

Refrigerated and frozen vegetarian foods, including tofu, bulk herbs, fresh nuts, grains, and a selection of packaged foods. Open Mon-Fri 9am-6pm, Sat 9:30am-5pm, closed Sun. Wednesday open until 8pm

Trader Joe's
15868 1st Ave S • Burien • (206) 901-9339 • www.traderjoes.com
See description – Seattle

FROM THE FARM

Burien Farmers' Market
Thursday, 11am-6pm, May-October
SW 152nd Street between 2nd & 6th SW
www.discoverburien.com

CARNATION

Carnation Farmers' Market
Tuesday, 3pm-7pm, May-September
SR 203-Tolt Avenue & Bird Street
www.carnationfarmersmarket.org

Full Circle Farm
NE 8th St • Carnation • (425) 333-4677
www.fullcirclefarm.com

One of Washington's largest Community-Supported Agriculture ventures, Full Circle partners with other farmers and artisan producers in Washington to bring more local food to market and to provide more variety in their CSA boxes. They offer a flexible membership program with three affordable box sizes, each containing a variety of nutritious organic produce consisting of a variety of fruits, vegetables, and herbs. Tours and various harvest celebrations are held throughout the year.

COVINGTON

Taco Del Mar
27116 168th Ave SE • Covington • (253) 630-4393 • www.tacodelmar.com
See review – Seattle

DES MOINES

Des Moines Farmers' Market on the Waterfront
Saturday, 10am-2pm, June-October
Des Moines Marina, S 227th St & Dock St
www.farmingandtheenvironment.org/DMFM

DUVALL

Duvall Farmers' Market
Wednesday, 3pm-7pm, June-September- except July 4
1st Avenue between Stella and Stephens St.
www.duvallfarmersmarket.com

EDMONDS

PCC Natural Markets
9803 Edmonds Way • Edmonds • Opening summer 2008
www.pccnaturalmarkets.com
See description – Seattle

Edmonds Museum Farmers' Market
Saturday, 9am-3pm, May-October
5th Ave N & Bell Street

EVERETT

DINING

Gorditos
1919 Hewitt Ave • Everett • (425) 252-4641
See review – Seattle

The Sisters
2804 Grand Ave • Everett • (425) 252-0480

VegFriendly • American • Mon-Fri breakfast & lunch • Closed Sat & Sun

This cozy family-owned-and-operated restaurant has walls covered with local artists' work. They offer buttermilk hotcakes, soups, salads, their own nut burger, hummus, and pita bread. Many menu items can be veggie upon request. Friendly, comfortable, informal setting.

Taco Del Mar
1723 Hewitt Ave • Everett • (425) 303-0300 • www.tacodelmar.com
See review – Seattle

SHOPPING

Sno Isle Natural Foods Co-op
2804 Grand Ave • Everett • (425) 259-3798 • www.snoislefoods.coop

A full service natural, organic and vegetarian grocery foods store with an extensive variety of vegan options as well as wheat-free and gluten-free foods. Excellent customer service. Deli and juice bar too! Open Mon-Sat 8am-8pm, Sun 12-6pm.

Trader Joe's
811 SE Everett Mall Way • Everett • (425) 513-2210 • www.traderjoes.com
See description – Seattle

FROM THE FARM

Everett Farmers' Market
Sunday, 11am-4pm, May-September
1600 W Marine View Drive at 16th Street
www.everettfarmersmarket.com

FEDERAL WAY

DINING

Taco Del Mar
1401 S 348th St • Federal Way • (253) 874-5842 • www.tacodelmar.com
2020 S 320th • Federal Way • (253) 839-9113
See review – Seattle

SHOPPING

Marlene's Market & Deli
2565 S Gateway Center Place • Federal Way • (253) 839-0933
www.marlenesmarket-deli.com

Marlene's carries an excellent selection of vegetarian food and is an important
resource for Federal Way and adjacent regions especially since its expansion a
couple of years ago. The aisles are easy to shop in and the staff is unusually helpful
and knowledgeable. There is a full organic produce section as well as a substantial
offering of meat and dairy substitutes. Shoppers will also find a good selection of
vitamins and supplements. On the second floor there is a delightful cafeteria with
many wholesome vegetarian selections. Parking is very convenient. Open Mon-Fri
8am-9pm, Sat 8am-8pm, Sun 10am-6pm.

Metropolitan Market
1618 Dash Point Rd • Federal Way • (206) 938-7020

Like the Tacoma store, a large, beautiful upscale market with a great selection of
vegan and vegetarian products. You'll find a salad bar, bulk bins, meat and cheese
analogs, nut butters, baby foods and frozen vegan and vegetarian foods as well as
health and beauty aids and organics. The Federal Way store also has deli with warm
and cold items such as pasta, fruit and vegetable salads and soups and sandwiches.
The produce department is expansive with higher quality produce than found in
most other stores, and the market boasts a very large fine wine department, including organic wines. All the employees are very friendly and knowledgeable.
Open 24 hours daily.

Trader Joe's
32073 Pacific Highway S • Federal Way • (253) 529-9242 • www.traderjoes.com
See description – Seattle

FIFE

Taco Del Mar
4617 Pacific Hwy • Fife • (253) 926-9564
See review – Seattle

ISSAQUAH

DINING

Acapulco Fresh
1480 NW Gilman Blvd • Issaquah • (425) 313-1542

VeryVegFriendly • Mexican • Daily lunch & dinner • Take out & counter ordering services

Using fresh ingredients daily and no lard, MSG, or can openers makes this Mexican fast- food restaurant a favorite for the health-conscious. The Baja Combo, vegetarian upon request, is a combination of grilled veggies, fajita style, with choice of corn or flour tortillas. With the rice, beans, sour cream, guacamole and chips on the side, a filling meal can be had for a very reasonable price. All-you-can-eat salsa bar. Whimsical southwest décor.

Bamiyan
317 NW Gilman Blvd • Issaquah • (425) 391-8081

VeryVegFriendly • Afghani cuisine • Daily lunch & dinner • Entrées $10-20

There is a separate vegetarian menu with six entrées. Very unique and tasty food. The Ashak dumplings, filled with scallions, cilantro, parsley and chives, are delightfully hot and spicy. The Badenjan Borani, fresh eggplant sautéed, baked and topped with tomato sauce, is delicious! Vegans: it's OK to bring your own soy yogurt for a topping as yogurt is used as a sauce extensively, but can easily be left off upon request.

Flying Pie Pizza
30 Front St S • Issaquah • (425) 391-2407 • www.flyingpiepizzeria.com

VegFriendly • Pizza • Daily lunch & dinner

First you choose the size of pizza, and whether the dough is whole-wheat or original (both are dairy- and egg-free). You select one of four crust styles, from extra thick (foccacia-style) to extra-thin (New-York-City-style), and specify your toppings, all freshly prepared that day. Vegan cheese is available. Play pinball while you wait for it to be cooked, then enjoy. Buy just a slice for lunch, or enjoy sharing a larger sized pizza. Half-and-halves are no problem. Ample parking and a diner style atmosphere make this a comfortable option for everyone.

Noodle Boat

700 NW Gilman Blvd • Issaquah • (425) 391-8096

VeryVegFriendly • Thai • Mon-Fri lunch • Daily dinner • Full service or take-out
Entrées $5-10

A delightful little restaurant located near the major shopping area on Gilman Blvd. Their food is delicious and light. In addition to their vegetarian menu, the staff is very helpful and receptive to creating vegan options. Outdoor seating is available during warmer weather.

Pabla Veggie Cuisine

1420 NW Gilman Blvd • Issaquah • (425) 392-4725
See review – Renton

SHOPPING

PCC Natural Markets

1810 12th Ave NW • Issaquah • (425) 369-1222 • www.pccnaturalmarkets.com
Open daily 6am -10pm
See description – Seattle

Trader Joe's

1495 11th Ave NW • Issaquah • (425) 837-8088 • www.traderjoes.com
See description – Seattle

KENMORE

Acapulco Fresh

6016 NE Bothell Way • Kenmore • (425) 482-0334
See review – Issaquah

Bastyr University Cafeteria

14500 Juanita Drive NE • Kenmore • (425) 823-1300 • www.bastyr.edu

Vegetarian • Cafeteria • Breakfast, lunch & dinner • Closed school holidays

Off the main path and in a university setting, anyone is welcome here for the all-vegetarian, frequently vegan cafeteria food. There is always a fresh salad bar, soup, and homemade baked breads and deserts. All this in the setting which has been the "heart of natural medicine for 25 years." Be sure to take a walk through their medicinal herb and vegetable gardens.

DINING

Chan Ho Vegetarian Restaurant
18124 E Valley Hwy • Kent • (425) 251-8818 • www.ChanHo.org

Vegetarian • Chinese • Daily lunch & dinner • Full service & take-out

Conveniently located between the Valley Medical Center and IKEA, just off Highway 167, you'll find the best Chinese vegetarian food in the south end at this clean and friendly restaurant. The food is always fresh and tasty. Enjoy a wide selection of tofu, vegetable and faux meat dishes, almost all of them vegan.

Circo Circo
23223 Pacific Highway S • Kent • (206) 878-4424

VegFriendly • Mexican • Daily lunch & dinner • Full service

The vegetarian co-owner ensures that you will find a vast selection of truly lard-free, simple and tasty vegetarian food. If you are vegan, ask them to hold the cheese. The vegetable fajitas are a great choice for vegans—hot and sizzling. The portions are huge and the décor down-home café. Very family-friendly.

Paulos
23810 104th Ave SE • Kent • (253) 850-2233

VegFriendly • Italian • Mon-Fri lunch • Daily dinner • Lunch $5-10 • Dinner $10-20

Italian food on the lighter side with a large number of vegetarian choices for the ovo-lacto vegetarian. Any pasta dish can be made meatless upon request. A vegan soup is sometimes offered. The antipasto plate or salad, minus the meat and cheese, is a particularly good choice. Ask your server for help in accommodating your diet choices.

Punjab Sweets
23617 104th Ave SE • Kent • (253) 859-3236

Vegetarian • Indian • Daily lunch & dinner

Authenticity and devotion to the vegetarian way seem to be the hallmarks of Punjab Sweets. They offer the largest selection of Indian deserts and sweets we have ever seen. This family-owned-and-operated restaurant also features a full menu of Indian vegetarian dishes and main course meals. Service is excellent and friendly. Already very popular among the region's growing Indian comunity, westerners are quickly discovering this restaurant as one of their favorites. A take-out menu and an ample and convenient parking lot are also available.

Spiro's Greek Island

215 1st Ave S • Kent • (253) 854-1030

VegFriendly • Greek • Mon-Sat lunch & dinner • Lunch $5-10 • Dinner $10-20
Closed Sun

The vegetarian choices are limited, but the food is good; the atmosphere is warm
and friendly. Try the Falafel Platter which can be extra-spicy. Baba Gannouj,
(smoked eggplant spread) and hummus (fava bean spread) are always good choices.
The pita bread is homemade, fresh and hot out of the oven. For vegans, hold the
feta cheese which is sprinkled on almost everything. Weekend nights there are colorful belly dancers, entertaining a packed house. Very child-friendly.

Taco Del Mar

21110 84th Ave S • Kent • (253) 395-1070 • www.tacodelmar.com
See review – Seattle

Wild Wheat Bakery

202 First Ave S • Kent • (253) 856-8919

VegFriendly • American • Daily breakfast & lunch • Entrées $5-10

About half the menu is, or could be, vegetarian. Vegetable soup is offered daily,
and other options include vegetable tempura, several entrée salads such as smoky-
lemon-and-honey salad with goat-cheese toast, roasted corn and black-bean salad,
roasted-pear-and-bleu-cheese salad with nuts, house salad with balsamic vinaigrette
(these are all large entrée salads). Also available is the wild-wheat vegetarian sandwich. Sunday brunch is always a treat with great traditional breakfast fare. Every
kind of baked dessert you can think of, freshly made by the pastry chef every morning.

Zao Noodle Bar

504 Ramsay Way • Kent • (253) 373 0414 • www.zao.com
See review – Seattle

FROM THE FARM

Kent Farmers' Market
Saturday, 9am-2pm, June-September
2nd and Harrison Streets

DINING

Café Happy
102 Kirkland Ave • Kirkland • (425) 822-9696

Vegetarian • Taiwanese-style Chinese • Lunch and dinner • Dine in or take out
Entrées under $6 • Cash only

A small, family-owned restaurant near the Kirkland waterfront. Excellent choice for vegetarian and vegan food, including vegetarian breakfasts and vegan lunches and dinners. Dishes are made fresh and light, with over 40 menu items to choose from. Descriptive pictures help the menu. They also serve dairy ice cream and have fresh-made juices and bubble teas.

Lakeshore Veggie House
15 Lake St #103 • Kirkland • (425) 889-2850 • www.bestveggiehouse.com

Vegetarian • Asian • Daily lunch & dinner • Full service • Entrées $5-10

The colored tablecloths and simple décor make this restaurant bright and cheery. Sit by the window for a view of Lake Washington, and enjoy a wide variety of Asian vegetarian food, from Chinese classics such as Won Ton Soup and House Special Chow Mein, to Malaysian Curry Pieces and Sushi.

Lucky Vegetarian Café
12069 124th Ave NE • Kirkland • (425) 820-8108

Vegetarian • Chinese • Mon-Sat breakfast, lunch & dinner • Closed Sun

Just south of the Totem Lake Mall is a small restaurant offering plentiful vegan Chinese fare. Protein options include veggie meatballs, soy ham, veggie fish or beef, and of course tofu. All the dishes are displayed as pictures so you can see what you'll be eating. Simple sandwiches with egg, cheese and veggie ham are also available, along with fresh juice blends, coffees, and teas.

Meze
935 6th St S • Kirkland • (425) 828-3923

VeryVegFriendly • Turkish Mediterranean • Breakfast, lunch & dinner • Closed Sun
Full service, take out and catering • Entrées $5-10

Virtually all the appetizers and many of the main dishes are vegetarian. One major favorite is panini with hummus, roasted eggplant, roasted red pepper, grilled onion, feta, and parsley. People rave about the falafel. Fresh-squeezed orange juice and lemonade and of course baklava in three flavors! Owner/chef Abraham loves to chat with customers.

Royal Indian Cuisine

9714 Juanita Drive NE • Kirkland • (425) 820-2303 • www.royalindiacuisine.com

VegFriendly • Indian • Daily lunch & dinner • Entrées $10-20

It's a delight to take your meat-eating friends out to dine at this authentic Indian restaurant. The sumptuous décor makes you feel like you're in an Indian palace. A wide selection of vegetarian entrees are available, such as Chana Masala (garbanzo curry), Aloo Gobi (potato and cauliflower curry), or Bhindi Masala (okra in spicy tomatoes). There's a buffet lunch available until 3pm, and you can order online for takeout. For a private party, reserve the luxurious tent room, which seats 20 on cushions around a low table.

Shamiana

10724 NE 68th St • Kirkland • (425) 827-4902

VegFriendly • Indian • Mon-Fri lunch • Daily dinner • Full service • Entrees $8-$12

With festive décor and family friendly smiles, Shamiana offers good service, delicious appetizers and moderate portions for all. The vegetarian menu is small but offers very tasty food with vegan options that include vegetable curry, eggplant dishes, and more.

Taco Del Mar

210 Main St Kirkland • (425) 827-0177 • www.tacodelmar.com
12551 116th Ave NE • Kirkland • (425) 820-5763
See review – Seattle

The Thai Kitchen

11701 124th Ave NE • Kirkland • (425) 820-5630

VeryVegFriendly • Thai • Daily lunch & dinner • Full service & take out • Entrées $5-10

The vegetarian menu has soup, appetizers and a few select entrées. The meals are served as spicy as you want and are flavorful. Friendly courteous staff provides fast service.

Thumra Thai Restaurant

12549 116th Ave NE (Totem Lake W) • Kirkland • (425) 821-0577

VegFriendly • Thai • Mon-Fri lunch • Daily dinner • Sat dinner only • Full service & take out • Entrées $5-10

This small, unassuming Thai restaurant just west of the Totem Lake exit off I-405 has no separate vegetarian menu. However, there is a highlighted area at the bottom of the menu stating that most dishes can be made using tofu or vegetables. The Tum Yum Soup was "yum in the tum" and had a spicy lemon grass base with tofu and mushrooms. Pud See Ewe, wide rice noodles with fried tofu and broccoli in a wonderful sauce, is a winner. The Pud Thai (Thailand's signature dish) was also done to perfection.

World Wrapps
124 Lake Street S • Kirkland • (425) 827-9727 • www.worldwrapps.com
See review – Bellevue

SHOPPING

PCC Natural Markets
10718 NE 68th • Kirkland • (425) 828-4622 • www.pccnaturalmarkets.com
Open daily 7am-11pm
See description – Seattle

Trader Joe's
12632 120th Ave NE • Kirkland • (425) 823-1685 • www.traderjoes.com
See description – Seattle

FROM THE FARM

Kirkland Farmers' Market
Wednesday, 12pm-6pm, May-October
Park Lane East between 3rd & Main

Friday, 3pm-7pm, June-October
Juanita Beach Park at 116th and 100th
www.kirklandwednesdaymarket.org

LAKE FOREST PARK

Third Place Commons Farmers' Market
Sunday, 11am-4pm, May-October
Bothell Way and Hwy 104

LAKEWOOD

Taco Del Mar
10417 Gravelly Lake Dr SW • Lakewood • (253) 584-8226
See review – Seattle

LYNNWOOD

DINING

Taco Del Mar
4201 196th St SW • Lynnwood • (425) 673-4607 • www.tacodelmar.com
See review – Seattle

Taster's Wok
15128 Highway 99 • Lynnwood • (425) 787-6789

VeryVegFriendly • Asian • Daily lunch & dinner • Full service & take out • Entrées $5-10

The separate vegetarian menu features a selection of dishes that use vegetable-product "fake" meats, including "chicken," "pork," and "salmon," as well as a wide selection of tofu dishes. Although the fake meat product contains egg whites, Taster's Wok is very accommodating to vegans and will substitute tofu in those particular dishes. It has a nice comfortable atmosphere and very friendly servers. It's a favorite for PAWS staff.

World Wrapps
3000 184th Street SW • Lynnwood • (425) 774-9727
See review – Bellevue

SHOPPING

Trader Joe's
19500 Highway 99 • Lynnwood • (425) 744-1346 • www.traderjoes.com
See description – Seattle

MILL CREEK

Taco Del Mar
1402 164th St SW • Mill Creek • (425) 743-5668 • www.tacodelmar.com
See review – Seattle

Central Market
15605 Main St • Mill Creek • (425) 357 3240 • www.millcreek.central-market.com
See review – Shoreline

MONROE

Taco Del Mar
19565 State Route 2 • Monroe • (360) 794-6560 • www.tacodelmar.com
See review – Seattle

MOUNTLAKE TERRACE

Manna Mills Natural Foods
21705 66th Ave W • Mountlake Terrace • (425) 775-3479

Pleasantly providing 100% organic produce and lots of dairy alternatives. Groceries are all-natural and mostly organic. They carry no commercial brands. Freezer section has a wide range of ready-to-cook meals. Open Mon-Fri 9am-8pm, Sat 9am-6pm, closed Sun.

MUKILTEO

DINING

La Cascada Acapulco

801 2nd St • Mukilteo • (425) 348-9569

VegFriendly • Mexican • Daily lunch & dinner • Entrées $5-10

The beautiful hand-painted scenes of Mexico surround you inside La Cascada, where a basket of chips and homemade salsa is on your table almost as soon as you sit down. There are many vegetarian options—vegan if you ask that they hold the cheese. This is one of the few Mexican restaurants around that doesn't use lard in their food. Black Bean Enchiladas are delicately spiced, with a red hot sauce on top. If you ask them, they'll even make vegan fajitas, and they are sizzling hot and fun to eat. At the end of the meal, they bring a complimentary deep-fried tortilla chip sprinkled with cinnamon sugar, topped with raspberry jam and a dollop of whipped cream.

Taco Del Mar

11700 Mukilteo Speedway Suite 406 • Mukilteo • (425) 493-1614
www.tacodelmar.com
See review – Seattle

FROM THE FARM

Mukilteo Farmers' Market

Wednesday, 3pm-7pm, June-September
Rosehill Community Center at 3rd & Lincoln
www.mukilteofarmersmarket.org

NORTH BEND

North Bend Farmers' Market

Thursday, 4pm-8pm, June-September
Si View Park (400 SE Orchard Dr)

PUYALLUP

DINING

Bangkok Thai Restaurant

520 39th Ave SW • Puyallup • (253) 445-8040

VeryVegFriendly • Thai • Daily lunch & dinner • Full service & take out

Family-owned and -staffed, you'll get the feeling that you're an honored guest in their home when you have a delicious vegetarian lunch or dinner. There is a section of the menu that is specifically vegetarian and any dish on the menu can be prepared for you with tofu substituting for other ingredients. Special requests are honored for vegan diners as the staff is sensitive to nutrition, religious or philosophical requirements. The portions are generous and served family-style.

Taco Del Mar

315 River Rd • Puyallup • (253) 435-5991 • www.tacodelmar.com
3827½ S Meridian Ave • Puyallup • (253) 841-7658
10929 Canyon Rd • Puyallup • (253) 537-1335
See review – Seattle

FROM THE FARM

Puyallup Farmers' Market

Saturday, 9am-2pm, May-October
Sunday, 10am-2pm, May-August
Pioneer Park & Pavilion, Meridian & 4th Avenue SW
www.puyallupmainstreet.com

REDMOND

DINING

Acapulco Fresh

16330 Cleveland St • Redmond • (425) 883-3510
See review – Issaquah

Haveli

16564 Cleveland St • Redmond • (425) 883-4443

VeryVegFriendly • Indian • Daily lunch (buffet) & dinner • Full service & take-out
Entrées $5-10

There are 21 vegetarian entrées on the menu plus many breads, some soups, and numerous appetizers that are meatless. Try the Saag Paneer and Eggplant Bhartha, both perfectly spiced, with fluffy basmati rice. The onion Kulcha (onion stuffed naan) was flavorful and filling. Have some chai tea for a perfect end to a comforting meal.

Mysore Masala

16650 Redmond Way • Redmond • (425) 558-7858

Vegetarian • South Indian • Daily lunch & dinner • Entrees $5-$10

A wide variety of Indian vegetarian options is offered, including South Indian classics such as Dosa, which is very popular. Try the all-you-can-eat lunch buffet or enjoy a delicious evening meal.

Preets
8440 160th Ave NE • Redmond • (425) 867 9400 • www.preets.com

Vegetarian • Indian • Daily lunch & dinner • Entrees $8-$11

The simple décor creates an understated elegance, which makes Preets a very popular place for lunch or dinner. The menu includes several creative versions of traditional Indian dishes, all beautifully presented. A few dishes are vegan, all others are vegetarian, and special requests can be accommodated.

Taco Del Mar
8074 160th Ave NE • Redmond • (425) 883-8822 • www.tacodelmar.com
14808 NE 24th St • Redmond • (425) 644-5055
See review – Seattle

Teapot Vegetarian House
5230 NE 24th St • Redmond • (425) 747-8881
www.teapotvegetarianhouse.com
See review – Seattle

SHOPPING

PCC Natural Markets
11435 Avondale Rd NE • Redmond • (425) 285-1400
www.pccnaturalmarkets.com • Daily 6am-10pm
See description – Seattle

Whole Foods Market
17991 NE Redmond Way • Redmond • (425) 881-2600
See description – Seattle

RENTON

DINING

Flying Pie Pizza
12642 164th Ave SE • Renton • (425) 228-8012 • www.flyingpiepizzeria.com
See review – Issaquah

Pabla Indian Cuisine
364 Renton Center Way SW • Renton • (425) 228-4625

Vegetarian & Kosher • East Indian • Daily lunch (buffet) & dinner • Full service
Entrées $5-10

One of the few vegetarian, kosher restaurants in the Seattle area. The cuisine is from the Punjab region of India and is deliciously, richly spiced. It's located in a little strip mall in Renton, and has typical strip mall décor. But don't let that fool you.

The food is great, and their lunch buffet is one of the best around. It usually has two or three vegan entrées, with many more lacto-vegetarian items. The Thali Dinners offer a sampling of eight or so dishes, and are a great alternative for those who like variety.

Taco Del Mar
20 SW 7th St • Renton • (425) 271-9594 • www.tacodelmar.com
4004 NE 4th St • Renton • (425) 271-8836
See review – Seattle

SHOPPING

Minkler's Green Earth
125 Airport Way • Renton • (425) 226-7757

Serving south King County since 1971 with quality natural foods and supplements at the lowest possible prices. They carry a huge selection of supplements, herbs, bulk foods, health and beauty aids and books. ——They also now carry natural and raw pet foods and pet supplements. Open Mon-Fri 9am-7pm, Sat 9:30am-6pm, closed Sun.

FROM THE FARM

Renton Farmers' Market
Tuesday, 3pm-7pm, June-September
S 3rd Street between Logan & Burnett
www.rentonfarmersmarket.com

SAMMAMISH

Acapulco Fresh
22830 NE 8th St • Sammamish • (425) 868-1447
See review – Issaquah

SEATAC

Bai Tong
15859 Pacific Highway S • Seatac • (206) 431-0893

VeryVegFriendly • Thai • Daily lunch and dinner • Entrées $5-10

Bai Tong is a northwest legend. It was originally opened to exclusively feed the crew from Thai Airways, with chefs brought in especially from Bangkok. For the last 10 years or so, it's been open to the rest of us, too. The food is fantastic, and very authentic. It is extremely vegetarian-friendly, with no fish sauce hidden in any menu item. There is a separate vegetarian menu but your choices are unlimited because almost any item on the menu can be made with tofu instead of meat. This place is a must-visit!

DINING

Agua Verde Paddle Club & Café

1303 NE Boat St • Seattle • (206) 545-8570 • www.aguaverde.com

VegFriendly • Mexican • Mon-Sat lunch & dinner • Closed Sun • Full service & take out • Entrees $5-$10

The choices for vegetarians are abundant, with no lard or other hidden animal ingredients. The Burrito Vegetariano is a favorite. So is the Tacos De Hongo (Portobello mushrooms, tomatoes, and onions sautéed with guajillo chiles and cotija cheese). The yam open-faced tacos are wonderful. Be sure to order some of their side dishes, like Pineapple Jicama Salsa. Delicious! A very inexpensive place for the entire family.

Araya's Vegetarian Place

1121 NE 45th St • Seattle • (206) 524-4332

Vegan • Thai • Daily lunch & dinner • Closed Sun • Full service, take-out, lunch buffet • Entrees $5-$10

When the only 100% vegan Thai restaurant in Seattle moved to its new location on 45th Street, it gained many more tables and a much more sophisticated style. It is still just as popular. Whether you prefer traditional Thai favorites such as Tom Kah soup or Bathing Rama, or more unusual dishes such as Taro Root A' La Bangkok or Avocado Curry, with more than 60 options on the menu to choose from, you're sure to find something to please. Choose as much as you can eat from the lunch buffet, or dine on specific menu choices in the evening.

Bahn Thai Restaurant

409 Roy St • Seattle • (206) 283-0444

VegFriendly • Thai • Daily lunch & dinner

Long a favorite part of Seattle's authentic Thai restaurant scene, Bahn Thai offers an extensive list of vegetarian and vegan entrées.

Bamboo Garden

364 Roy Street • Seattle • (206) 282-6616 • www.bamboogarden.net

Vegan & Kosher • Chinese • Daily lunch & dinner • Full service & take out Entrées $5-10

When asked "So what do vegans eat," bring them here. They will be deliciously overwhelmed with over 100 menu items, all vegan and all kosher. There are creative and traditional Chinese sauces, crisp veggies, thick doughy noodles, and faux meats that are so real you will keep checking the menu just to be sure. Soft chatter and quick moving servers let you know that you are in a popular place without feeling crowded.

Big Bowl Noodle House

814 NE 65th St • Seattle • (206) 985-6855 • www.bigbowlnoodle.com

VeryVegFriendly • Thai • Daily lunch & dinner • Entrées $5-10

A tiny gem a bit north of the University of Washington, Big Bowl serves huge portions of Phad Thai, always wonderful and less sweet than most Thai restaurants. It's hard not to always re-order the Vegetarian M-80 – a huge bowl of spicy soup noodles (choice of egg, thin or thick rice noodles) full of tofu plus many veggies. Fresh or fried, the spring rolls are amazing and the service is the best! It's a family affair and spotlessly clean.

The Cafe by Hillside Quickies

324 15th Ave E • Seattle • (206) 325-6429 • www.hillsidequickie.com

Vegan • Eclectic • Mon-Sat lunch & dinner • Closed Sun

Delicious vegan pizzas, burgers, soups, sandwiches and wraps are uniquely created in this small café on Capitol Hill. Smoked barbecue tofu, Jamaican spice tempeh, grilled tofustrami, and breaded seitan are just a few of the innovative flavors on offer in their burgers, wraps, and sandwiches. Pizza offerings, available by the slice, vary each day. Sister café to Hillside Quickie's Sandwich Shop in the University District.

Café Flora

2901 East Madison • Seattle • (206) 325-9100 • www.caféflora.com

Vegetarian • Gourmet • Daily lunch & dinner • Entrées $10-20

Although all of Café Flora's menu is completely vegetarian, many non-vegetarians are repeat customers coming to enjoy more fine gourmet dinners. The dishes are prepared using seasonal vegetables and although the menu changes regularly, there are always standard options such as the French dip sandwich and the curry (veg) burger. The presentation of dishes is outstanding and very colorful. The interior is decorated with vibrant colors, new artists' work is displayed throughout, and the interior atrium with seating around a fountain creates a very pleasant atmosphere. Popular Sunday brunch.

California Pizza Kitchen

401 NE Northgate Way • Seattle • (206) 367-4445 • www.cpk.com
See review – Bellevue

Carmelita

7314 Greenwood Ave N • Seattle • (206) 706-7703 • www.carmelita.net

Vegetarian • Eclectic • Dinner only • Closed Mon • Full service • Entrées $15-20

Gourmet vegetarian cuisine at this popular Phinney Ridge bistro with vegan alternatives for every course. Excellent service and great selection of food. Desserts served in generous portions, enough to share.

Chaco Canyon

4759 Brooklyn Ave NE • Seattle • (206) 522-6966

Vegan • American • Daily breakfast, lunch & dinner • Cafeteria • Entrees $5-$10

The food is 100% vegan and 95% organic ingredients at Chaco Canyon Organic Cafe. Their menu features American-style cuisine, with occasional ethnic options such Thai, Indian, and Mediterranean. Restaurant specialties include a generous selection of juices and smoothies. Menu options fall into two main groupings: uncooked for those following a raw-foods diet and cooked for conventional vegetarians. The informal dining atmosphere is cheerful, with Native-American touches.

Chutneys

1815 N 45th St • Seattle • (206) 634 1000 • www.chutneysbistro.com
See review – Bellevue

Cyber Dogs

909 Pike St • Seattle • (206) 405-3647 • www.cyber-dogs.com

Vegetarian • Hot dogs • Daily till late • Full service & take out • Entrees $5-7

Giving a new reputation to the hot dog, these are all vegetarian, mostly vegan, totally crazy and absolutely yummy. Start the day with a Breakfast Dog (served all day) like the Banana Dog, or the Bratwurst (ovo-vegetarian), topped with breakfast-type things like vegetarian bacon or hollandaise sauce. There are also pastries and gourmet coffees. Later try the Laika Dog, with Russian Eggplant Caviar. Or the DoggiLama with masala and Cumber Yogurt Sauce. And it's all wrapped up in an art-filled internet café. Fantastic!

Elysian Brewing Company

1221 E Pike St • Seattle • (206) 860-1920 • www.elysianbrewing.com
542 1st Ave S • Seattle • (206) 382-4498
2106 N 55th St • Seattle • (206) 547-5929

VegFriendly • PubGrub • Daily lunch & dinner • Entrées $5-10

A great choice for a vegetarian or vegan in the mood for a microbrew experience. About a third of the menu is made of great vegetarian, mostly vegan choices, with usually a vegan soup of the day. Sandwiches feature Field Roast, a lentil-based meat substitute in a variety of tangy sauces, and there are old favorites like rice and beans, veggie burgers, and pasta. The Elysian also brews many varieties of its draft beers (vegan!) Try the beer sampler tray or non-alcoholic Elysian root beer and ginger beer.

Enat Ethiopian Restaurant

11546 15th Ave NE • Seattle • (206) 362-4901

VegFriendly • Ethiopean • Tues-Sun lunch & dinner • Closed Mon • Full service & take-out • Entrees $5-$10

This family-friendly restaurant offers a delicious Vegetarian Combo platter, with

Injera bread (made from teff) served with various vegetable- and lentil-dish samples. There's too much for one person to eat, so share it with a friend or plan to take some home. The spice level is mild, which makes it comfortable for most people. Many non-vegetarians choose this platter in preference to meat-based dishes. The restaurant has plenty of easy parking.

Flowers Bar and Restaurant
4247 University Way NE • Seattle • (206) 633-1903

Vegan • American • Daily lunch buffet $8

An amazing hot-and-cold-buffet of 30 items, all-vegan pastas, curries, soups, faux-creamed cauliflower, steamed green-bean-and-broccoli mélange, several hot spinach dishes, and several salads—all for eight bucks! Bright, natural daytime light by full glass walls on two sides and mirrored ceiling. Happily painted tables. A pleasant flow of customers, maybe 50% purpose-driven student, yet plenty of space for a lengthy, casual mid-day adult conversation. Evening meals are definitely not vegetarian, being mainstream with an active, full bar.

Georgetown Liquor Company
5501B Airport Way S • Seattle • (206) 763-6764
www.georgetownliquorcompany.com

Vegetarian • Eclectic • Mon-Fri lunch • Daily dinner till late • Entrees $9-$12

The rumble and the occasional whistle from a nearby train track won't be enough to distract you from the fare at Georgetown Liquor Company–it's that good. The vegetarian entrées and gourmet sandwiches are quite colorful. The enchilada and tamale plates are a hearty, healthy, and tasty alternative, and sandwiches like the Frac, made with lentil-sage Field Roast, apricot chutney, primrose brie, and fresh Roma tomatoes, are unique and mouth-watering treats. All entrées and sandwiches can be made vegan. Don't miss the vintage video games by the door!

Gorditos
213 N 85th St • Seattle • (206) 706-9352

VegFriendly • Mexican • Daily lunch & dinner • Cafeteria & take-out • Entrees $5-$10

This fun and lively restaurant is very authentically Mexican, with abundant affordable food, and plenty of seating for everyone. The Veggie Veggie burrito is delicious, and huge—plenty for two people. Ask for the Chicito option if you prefer a regular-sized burrito. Many other burritos are available with tofu, served fajita-style. The beans they serve contain no lard or oil, the rice doesn't include chicken stock, the guacamole contains no dairy, and the salsas are made from fresh tomatoes and chilies.

Hillside Quickie's Shop

4106 Brooklyn Ave • Seattle • (206) 632-3037

Vegan-organic • Eclectic • Mon-Sat lunch & dinner

Intentionally low-key but notably high-profile sandwiches made from homemade seitan, tempeh, or tofu. Raves for their Crazy Jamaican Burger, which is grilled plantain, onions, and tofu. Famous is their Macaroni & Yease, and the seitan "steak," mashed potatoes and vegan gravy. A brunch suggested is the polenta and vegan French toast. The foods created and offered by this African-American family go on and on. See the Tacoma listing for Quickie Too.

In the Bowl Vegetarian Noodle Bistro

1554 E Olive Way • Seattle • (206) 568-2343

Vegetarian • Thai • Daily lunch & dinner • Entrees $5-$10

Situated on one of the best people-watching streets on Capitol Hill, In the Bowl is a small but colorful bistro that goes beyond tofu to feature various soy "meat" ana-logs, among them soy chicken, beef, duck, fish, and prawn. The extensive menu is thoughtfully arranged into various "episodes," ranging from the "starter" (appetizer) episode to the salad, soup, noodle, curry, fried rice, and stir-fried episodes. Standout dishes include Spicy Coconut Milk Noodle with prawns and Roasted Duck Curry. The "spiciness" scale is skewed toward heat—a medium-spicy request might make your eyes water!

Jhanjay

1718 N 45th St • Seattle • (206) 632-1484 • www.jhanjay.com

Vegetarian • Thai • Daily lunch & dinner • Full service & take out • Entrées $5-10

Located on Wallingford's fashionable 45th Street, this gem of a restaurant serves some of the best Thai food available. Try Monk's Noodles, just one of the 16 choices available for lunch, served with vegetables, tofu (fried or steamed) and a bowl of the soup of the day. In the evening, there are endless delicious options to choose from, all served with tofu or veggie meat. Sit up at the counter and watch the chef prepare your food, or relax at one of the many small tables in this warm and cosy restaurant.

Juliano's Pizza

1211 Pine St • Seattle • (206) 625-9922

VeryVegFriendly • Pizza • Daily lunch & dinner

Plenty of vegan options are available at this small pizza bar, just over I-5 from the main downtown area. Each pizza is made fresh to order, even though you can buy just a small slice if you like. Get take-out or sit at bar stools and enjoy. Open till the early hours of the morning, this is a great place to get a tasty late-night snack.

Kabul Afghan Cuisine

2301 N 45th • Seattle • (206) 545-9000

VeryVegFriendly • Afghani • Daily dinner only

Five time winner at "Bite of Seattle." A unique culinary experience, bringing a subtle blend of spices, home recipes, and photography to transport you to the Afghan city of Kabul. Try the Bolani Turnovers with herbs, potatoes and tomato sauce; Shornakhod: chickpeas and kidney beans in a lemon-vinegar dressing; Qorma-I Tarkari: cauliflower, carrots and potato with dill, turmeric and cumin; Bodenjan Borani: eggplant with tomato sauce and mint. The mango sorbet dessert is specially made for Kabul. Wine available. Live sitar music some nights.

Kitaro Japanese Cuisine

1624 N 45th St • Seattle • (206) 547-7998

VeryVegFriendly • Japanese • Mon-Sat lunch & dinner • Wed lunch only • Sun dinner only • Entrées $7-13

Vegetarian sushi is the specialty of this wonderful Japanese restaurant, with about 20 different vegetarian choices such as burdock root or tofu with garlic and avocado. Every dish on the extensive menu can be made vegetarian by substituting tofu for meat where necessary. There are also noodle soups, stir-fry noodles, and many vegetarian rice dishes such as the vegetables-and-tofu teriyaki, all available with brown rice if you prefer.

Kwanjai Thai

469 N 36th St • Seattle • (206) 632-3656

VeryVegFriendly • Thai • Daily lunch & dinner • Full service & take-out • Entrées $5-10

The restaurant, run by a Thai family, is situated inside a tiny house where the atmosphere is bursting with energy, yet it is very cozy as all the tables are placed close together. The food comes quickly, and most entrées can be prepared vegetarian by omitting the fish sauce and asking for tofu instead of meat. A favorite dish is the eggplant with tofu.

Lucky Palate

307 W McGraw St • Seattle • (206) 352-2583 • www.luckypalate.com

Vegetarian • Eclectic • Home delivery, take out & storefront meals

A popular home-delivery service of delicious gourmet vegetarian or vegan meals on a weekly basis. Choose from two to six meals per week, with or without dessert, or order a la carte. The storefront is open off and on for grab-and-go meals and a selection of homemade groceries.

Mighty-O Donuts

2110 N 55th St • Seattle • (206) 547-0335 • www.mightyo.com

Vegan • Donut & coffee shop • Breakfast thru lunch • Sit in or take out

These are big, rich cake donuts, so moist, dense and delicious that you will be reminded why you drink coffee in the first place. A friendly neighborhood coffee house, with some sandwiches and juices, newspaper strewn tables, comfy chairs, couches, soothing folk music, and excellent espresso. Try the chocolate coconut. Unbelievable!

Moonlight Café

1919 S Jackson St • Seattle • (206) 322-3378

VeryVegFriendly • Vietnamese • Daily lunch & dinner

The Moonlight Cafe, situated at the edge of Seattle's International District, features oriental cuisine and a separate vegetarian menu. This is one of the most extensive vegetarian menus we have seen in a non-vegetarian restaurant with well over 100 selections, most of which are vegan. Service is attentive, take out is available and a small parking lot is available. Becoming popular by word of mouth, we are happy to put in print what so many already know.

Patty Pan Grill

5402 20th Ave NW • Seattle • (206) 782-1558
Also at various local Farmers' Markets

Vegetarian • Northwest • Mon-Sat lunch & take out • Closed Sunday

Primarily for take-out, Patty Pan is nonetheless a great place to enjoy lunch on a sunny day in Seattle. A small bar at the window provides seating for those rainy days. This is a small and good-natured grill, where culinary wonders are worked and the food is hearty and made with care. Special attention is given to savory blends of spices and fresh, local ingredients. The vegan tamales alone are well worth the trek to Ballard. Be sure to take home some tomatillo salsa—you'll be craving it later.

Phoenecia at Alki

2716 Alki Ave SW • Seattle • (206) 935-6550

VegFriendly • Mediterranean • Dinner only • Closed Mon • Full service • Entrées $10-20

On Alki beach in West Seattle, offering several options for vegetarians, such as salads, pizza, and pasta dishes. Instead of relying strictly on the menu, let Phoenicia's owner, Chef Hussein Khazaal, select a dish for you which can be a vegetable curry entrée as a very flavorful and satisfying vegan meal.

Pizza Pi

5500 University Way NE • Seattle • 206-343-1415

Vegan • Pizza • Tues-Fri dinner • Sat-Sun lunch & dinner • Closed Mon

Vegans rejoice—finally there is a cheese-free pizzeria! Pizza Pi features vegan pizzas with all the extras. The atmosphere is informal. Allow a few extra minutes for cooking, as everything is made fresh. Take out is available. Remember to bring a few quarters for pinball.

Quazis Indian Curry House
473 N 36th St • Seattle • (206) 632-3575

VegFriendly • Indian • Daily lunch & dinner • Full service & take out • Entrées $5-10

This restaurant serves a superb Eggplant Bharta (request without cream if vegan). Their Vegetable Pakoras are vegan, as are the Spinach Naan and Aloo Paratha, very welcome since in most restaurants naan bread is not vegan. Opened in 2002, the atmosphere is quiet. Seats are surrounded by vases on the wall with fabric undulating above and across the walls.

Rovers
2808 E Madison St • Seattle • (206) 325-7442 • www.rovers-seattle.com

Vegfriendly • Dinner only • Closed Sun-Mon • 5-course set menu • Full service Must reserve

High-end, exclusive restaurant offers one 8-course and two 5-course set menus, one of which is always vegetarian. The menus change slightly every day, and with 24-hours notice, they can provide a vegan menu. Set back behind the storefronts on the west side of Madison Street, you will feel like you have walked into a private house as you enter the several small cozy rooms of the dining area. While the portions are small, each course is exquisitely presented and very flavorful. By the time you've enjoyed all five dishes, plus a dessert plate and tea or coffee, you will feel comfortably satisfied and delightfully indulged.

Shalimar Pakistani & Indian Cuisine
4214 University Way • Seattle • (206) 633-3854

VeryVegFriendly • Pakistani & Indian • Mon-Sat lunch & dinner

Spacious and ethnically decorative, Shalimar has a major vegetarian (but not vegan) menu with over half of the extensive list of dishes being all South-Asian vegetarian. Some specialties are Shulgam Palak, a simmer of turnips and spinach in tomato sauce, Bengan Ki Bahji, which is slow cooked eggplant in a curry, and Aloo Gobi, cauliflower and potatoes simmered in "delightful" spices. Lassis and chais to sip or vegan beer & wines.

Silence Heart Nest
3508 Fremont Pl N • Seattle • (206) 633-5169 • www.silenceheartnest.com

Vegetarian • Eclectic • Wed-Mon breakfast & lunch • Closed Tues • Full service

Enjoy delicious vegetarian pancakes, waffles, and eggs-and-tofu scrambles for breakfast. For lunch, options vary from veggie burgers and sandwiches, burritos and curries, to their ever-famous "Neat Loaf" with mashed potatoes and gravy. All are delicious and presented with warmth and caring by Sri Chinmoy devotees.

Snappy Dragon

8917 Roosevelt Way NE • Seattle • (206) 528-5575 • www.snappydragon.com

Very Veg-friendly • Chinese • Mon-Sat lunch • Daily dinner • Full service, take out, catering & delivery • Entrées $5-10

Ask for the special vegetarian menu at this popular Chinese restaurant. Judy Fu, the owner, is one of the most highly respected Chinese chefs in Seattle, and her restaurant is renowned for the Mandarin/Szechuan style of cooking. Try her special vegetarian potstickers as an appetizer. Asparagus in Black Bean Sauce is one of her signature dishes, and the Ma Po Tofu is delicious. On a busy night, make a reservation ahead of time, or order takeout. They'll even deliver if you live nearby.

Sound View Café

1501 Pike Pl • Seattle • (206) 623-5700

VegFriendly • Cafeteria • Daily breakfast, lunch & early dinner

Located downstairs in the Pike Place Market, this health-minded restaurant has an unusual variety of vegetarian specialties. Enjoy watching the ferries in Puget Sound while sitting on a stool by the window, enjoying great food!

Squid & Ink

1128 S Albro Pl • Seattle • (206) 763-2696

Vegan • Eclectic • Tues-Sun breakfast, lunch & dinner

A creative part of the revitalization of the Georgetown neighborhood, Squid & Ink is well worth seeking out. With a distinctive style, the Squid's meals are delicious, the service is attentive and friendly, and the prices are reasonable. They serve breakfast until 4pm—try the vegan French toast or Greek "ohmlette." For dinner, treat yourself to a hearty, seitan-based chicken-fried steak or Maple Teriyaki Fish. For a unique snack any time of day, try the vegan poutine!

Sunlight Café

6403 Roosevelt Way NE • Seattle • (206) 522-9060

Vegetarian • Ethnic eclectic • Daily breakfast, lunch & dinner • Full service • Entrées $5-10

One of the first vegetarian restaurants in Seattle and still a relaxed setting with tasty selections. A good casual meeting place and excellent value.

Taco Del Mar

1033 65th NE • Seattle • (206) 729-0670 • www.tacodelmar.com
12311 Lake City Way NE • Seattle • (206) 363-9151
3526 Fremont Pl N • Seattle • (206) 545-8001
8004 Greenwood Ave N • Seattle • (206) 706-4063
6101 15th Ave NW • Seattle • (206) 297-4446
725 Pike St • Seattle • (206) 628-8982
1165 Harrison St • Seattle • (206) 624-2114
1520 Broadway • Seattle • (206) 328-4868
107 1st Ave • Seattle • (206) 467-5940
2136 1st Ave • Seattle • (206) 448-8877
823 Third Ave • Seattle • (206) 467-4878
2932 4th Ave S • Seattle • (206) 521-8887
2401 Utah Ave S • Seattle • (206) 343-0552
4740 42nd Ave SW • Seattle • (206) 938-1413
830 NE Northgate Way • Seattle • (206) 267-6767
1313 NE 42nd St • Seattle • (206) 547-2390
29 W Mercer St • Seattle • (206) 216-5990
411 Cedar St • Seattle • (206) 443-4300
908 Stewart St • Seattle • (206) 624-4300
1620 4th Ave • Seattle • (206) 343-0400
2309 S Jackson St • Seattle • (206) 329-8383
2600 SW Barton St • Seattle • (206) 938-6694

VeryVegFriendly • Lunch & dinner • Entrées under $5.

Vegan fast food? Yes, it's true! Try Taco Del Mar for a colorful, fun restaurant known for fresh and quality ingredients as well as a healthy fast food alternative. There are many vegetarian options and a vegan burrito right on the menu. Don't forget to try the smoothies and the chips and salsa, as they are excellent. The friendly staff will quickly prepare your food right in front of you. Perfect for kids.

Tawon Thai

3410 Fremont Ave • Seattle • (206) 633-4545 • www.tawonthai.com

VeryVegFriendly • Thai • Daily lunch & dinner

Their new vegetarian menu offers a surprising number of appetizers, soups and en-trées made without eggs or fish sauce. For a wonderful Thai feast, try the savory Pad Woon Sen, stir fried bean thread noodles with pineapple, celery, green onion, nappa cabbage, bell peppers, and tofu, or the Pad Kee Mou, stir fried wide noodles with broccoli, tomatoes, basil, and chili sauce. There are great desserts to choose from, such as sweet black sticky rice in coconut milk, coconut, mango ice cream, and the tasty pairing of white rice and mango.

Teapot Vegetarian House

345 15th Ave E • Seattle • (206) 325-1010

Vegan & Kosher • Asian • Daily lunch & dinner • Full service & take-out • Entrées $5-10

Many of the Teapot menu items feature mock meat dishes. Start a meal with their spring rolls or the mushroom-and-lettuce appetizer. The very popular Rose drum-mettes are served with a table-brightening sweet-and-sour sauce. There are a variety of Asian favorites, like Yaki Udon, Szechuan "Beef," and an array of soy-based stir fries. The "Rama Garden" of fresh veggies are steamed to crisp perfection and served with a tofu-and-peanut sauce. The thick "House Noodles", with the heaping pile of vegetables is a local favorite. Count on a healthy, hearty meal at a moderate price. The ambience is very relaxing. Live music is featured on Saturday nights.

Thai Kitchen

2220 Queen Anne Ave • Seattle • (206) 285-8424

VeryVegFriendly • Thai • Daily lunch & dinner • Full service & take out • Entrées $5-10

A very pleasant ambience in the living room of an old house, with lots of outdoor seating as well. The Thai spices are subtle but pleasant. Pud Thai and Yellow Curry are excellent. There are about 35 vegetarian choices and the service is fine and prompt.

Vegan Garden

1228 S Jackson St • Seattle • (206) 726-8669

Vegan • Vietnamese • Daily lunch & dinner • Closed Tues • Full service & take-out

The Vegan Garden, located in Seattle's International District, is one of the region's newest restaurants and has become an instant success. The menu features authentic Vietnamese and Pan Asian cuisine, and it includes faux meats so real you'll be double checking that you're in the right restaurant. Also available is an excellent selection of traditional dishes. The atmosphere is pleasant and the service is excellent. A take-out menu is available. Parking is plentiful.

Vegetarian Bistro

668 King St • Seattle • (206) 624-8899

Vegetarian • Chinese • Daily lunch & dinner • Closed Tues
Full service & take-out

The International District in Seattle is home to some of the finest and most authen-tic Chinese restaurants in the Pacific Northwest. The atmosphere at the Vegetarian Bistro is both elegant and relaxing, and the food is epicurean. The owner, originally from Hong Kong and now something of a celebrity in the vegetarian community, spares no effort to make each dish authentic and satisfying. The menu features a careful selection of both the most innovative and traditional dishes, with vegetarian Dim Sum a signature dish. The service is excellent. There's also a take-out menu for those on the run.

Veggie Veggie

4537 University Way NE • Seattle • (206) 547-6500

Vegetarian • Thai • Daily lunch & dinner • Full service and take-out
Entrees $5-$10

Veggie Veggie features authentic Thai cuisine. Portions are quite generous and the lunch specials are an especially good deal. Most menu options are vegan. Try one of the dishes with the soy "beef." It tasted so real it had us double-checking to make sure we were in the right place! The dishes are flavorful instead of merely spicy. Brown rice is available. The service is attentive. The atmosphere is modern, complete with contemporary Thai music and soap operas on the big screen. Take-out is available.

Wayward Café

901 NE 55th Street • Seattle • (206) 524-0204 • www.myspace.com/waywardcafe

Vegan • Homestyle • Tues-Sun, breakfast & lunch • Closed Mon

A Bohemian atmosphere characterizes this small, worker-owned-and-operated Seattle restaurant. At the Wayward, you'll find stick-to-your-ribs vegan fare at reasonable prices. The menu features traditional dishes made vegan and the taste is quite satisfying. Portions are most generous, a welcome respite from nouvelle cuisine, so remember to bring your appetite.

World Wrapps

528 Queen Ann Ave N • Seattle • (206) 286-9727 • www.worldwrapps.com
1109 Madison St • Seattle • (206) 467-9744
7900 E Greenlake Drive • Seattle • (206) 524-9727
2750 NE University Village • Seattle • (206) 522-7873
222 Yale Ave N • Seattle • (206) 233-0222
601 Union St • Seattle • (206) 628-9601
400 Pine St • Seattle • (206) 628-6868
701 5th Ave-Columbia Tower • Seattle • (206) 340-0810
801 Alaskan Way • Seattle • (206) 621-9727
See review – Bellevue

Zao Noodle Bar

2590 University Village • Seattle • (206) 529-8278 • www.zao.com

VeryVegFriendly • Asian noodle bar • Daily lunch & dinner • $5-10

"Health & Wisdom in a Bowl" portends the complex, balanced flavors in their noodle bowls, but start off with a vegan appetizer like Crispy Tofu Fries with three sauces or Roasted Wasabi Peas. Entrées have innovative ingredients like soy-lime dressing. The Monk's Vegetarian Delight or the Vietnamese Rice Noodles with Five Vegetables is recommended. Portions are huge and the food is "scrumptious."

SHOPPING

Madison Market

1600 E Madison • Seattle • (206) 329-1545 • www.madisonmarket.com

One of the newer, "super-natural" food stores. Friendly, upbeat, and community-based in a modern setting. A member-based co-op open to the public. Broad selection of natural foods, meat substitutes, soy products, frozen and packaged goods, bulk products, and of course a huge selection of organic produce. Very responsive to customers' requests. In-store deli with fresh kitchen delights daily. Animal-friendly health and beauty aids. Wide selection of vegetarian books and magazines. Open daily 7am-midnight

Metropolitan Market

1908 Queen Anne Ave N • Seattle • (206) 284-2530
100 Mercer St • Seattle • (206) 213-0778
2320 42nd Ave SW • Seattle • (206) 937-0551
5250 40th Ave NE • Seattle • (206) 938-6600
See review – Federal Way

Mother Nature's Nutrition

516 Queen Ann Ave N • Seattle • (206) 284-4422

In small print the sign says "Vitamins/Cosmetics," but once inside you find herbs, sports supplements, and a small bar for smoothies and juices, home-cooked take-out soups, and sandwiches. A small, friendly store. No fresh veggies, but some frozen "natural" foods and of course soy milks. Open Mon-Fri 9:30-7pm, Sat 9:30-6pm, closed Sun.

New Roots Organics

Seattle • (206) 261-2500 • www.newrootsorganics.com

They will deliver a bin of 12 to 15 fruits and veggies to your door weekly in Seattle, Bellevue, and Kirkland. First source suppliers seasonally are from Washington organic growers.

PCC Natural Market-Fremont

600 N 34th • Seattle • (206) 632-6811 • www.pccnaturalmarkets.com
Daily 6am-midnight

PCC Natural Market-Greenlake

7504 Aurora Ave N • Seattle • (206) 525-3586 • Daily 7am-11pm

PCC Natural Market-Seward Park

5041 Wilson Ave S • Seattle • (206) 723-2720 • Daily 7am-10pm

PCC Natural Market-View Ridge

6514 40th Ave NE • Seattle • (206) 526-7661 • Daily 7am-11pm

PCC Natural Market-West Seattle
2749 California Ave SW • Seattle • (206) 937-8481 • Daily 7am-11pm

PCC is the leader of the natural/organic food movement in the Puget Sound region. From its roots 50 years ago, this co-op will soon have nine locations in the greater Seattle area. PCC pioneered many of the policies in the natural/organic food grocery movement that are now recognized as standards. In all departments, you can find products that were produced without synthetic chemicals, additives, or genetically modified ingredients. Effort is made to select sustainable crops, fairly traded and humanely grown or manufactured foods or products. All stores offer the finest Northwest farm-fresh produce, with many locally grown organic fruits and vegetables. Every store's deli has delicious, made-from-scratch salads and entrees ready to take home or have catered. The bulk food area offers all manner of beans, grains, flours, oils, sweeteners, herbs and teas. The body care products are based on natural botanical ingredients. As a co-op, PCC addresses various consumer food or industry concerns to legislators and other decision makers with the collective voice of its 40,000 members. Member benefits include a special 10-percent-off coupon each month, home delivery of the monthly paper with articles on consumer food concerns and co-op education, and discounts on Foodworks classes, PCC's cooking-and-nutrition program. PCC's community programs include a Kids Club, and it is the largest corporate sponsor of the PCC Farmland Fund, a nonprofit land trust that preserves endangered farmland for organic production.

Pioneer Organics
901 NW 49th St • Seattle • (206) 632-3424 • www.pioneerorganics.com

From Tacoma to Everett and east to the Sammamish Plateau, Pioneer can deliver various-sized boxes of fresh, certified organic fruits and vegetables to your door. They will also deliver a wide range of breads and groceries and welcome special orders.

Sidecar for Pigs Peace
5270B University Way NE • Seattle • (206) 523-9060

Imagine a totally vegan grocery store because that's what you'll find at Sidecar. This is the place to look for hard-to-find items. Although Sidecar is a small store, the selection is impressive. Everything from vegan marshmallows to leather-free shoes and belts can be found at this store. Even better, all the proceeds go to benefit the nonprofit farm-animal sanctuary, Pig's Peace. Open Tues-Sun 10am- 8pm. Closed Mon.

Trader Joe's
112 W Galer St • Seattle • (206) 378-5536 • www.traderjoes.com
4555 Roosevelt Way NE • Seattle • (206) 547-6299
1700 Madison St • Seattle • (206) 322-7268

"TJ's" is a unique chain of medium-sized grocery stores often in tucked-away locations. You'll find a treasure of interesting products, mostly packaged, canned, or bottled. There is a small but well-stocked fresh vegetable section and plenty of faux meats in the cooler or freezer. The kosher label will be found on an extensive number of products in virtually all categories. Many of the foods are private labeled with their own "angle," i.e., vegetarian, organic, or just plain decadent. All have minimally processed ingredients from a variety of suppliers, many international, who make interesting products often exclusive to this chain. Known for generally low prices, there is a whole underground of wine aficionados who set price/value standards by TJ's bargain bottles. Open daily 9am-9pm.

Uwajimaya Village

600 5th Ave S • Seattle • (206) 624-6248 • www.uwajimaya.com

The new Uwajimaya Village is a shopping experience that must be seen to be believed. The store is enormous and chock full of the Asian specialties, teas, and spices that vegetarians and vegans love. The produce section is large and well stocked with many otherwise hard to find fruits and vegetables. Asian meat analogs as well as some brand-name food items. The food court has 7 restaurants and a store deli, each with several vegetarian and vegan options. Open daily 9am-10pm.

Whole Foods Market

1026 NE 64th • Seattle • (206) 985-1500 • www.wholefoods.com
2210 Westlake Ave • Seattle • (206) 621-9700

Whole Foods presents natural foods in a big, clean, contemporary, brightly lit, one-stop environment. The vegetable/fruit section is like walking into a large, colorful, mostly organic garden, glistening with dew. There is a large selection of healthy faux meats. All products sold are free of trans-fat containing hydrogenated oils. There are quality alternative brands of non-food products. Extensive and tempting presentation of ready-to-eat hot foods and salad bar with seating area. Great wine selection. Prices tend to be high, but so is the quality and selection. The employees here are upbeat and helpful. Open daily 8am-10pm.

FROM THE FARM

Ballard Farmers' Market

Sunday, 10am-4pm (Winter 11am-3pm), open year-round
Ballard Avenue NW between 20th NW & 22nd NW
www.seattlemarkets.org

Broadway Sunday Farmers' Market

Sunday, 11am-3pm, May-November
Broadway & E Thomas
www.seattlefarmersmarkets.org

Columbia City Farmers' Market

Wednesday, 3pm-7pm, May-October
4801 Rainier Avenue S at Edmunds Street
www.seattlefarmersmarkets.org

Lake City Farmers' Market
Thursday, 3pm-7pm, May-October
NE 127th Street & 30th Avenue NE
www.seattlefarmersmarkets.org

Mad Cap Farmers' Market
Friday, 3pm-7pm, May-September
East Union and MLK Jr. Way
www.seattlemarkets.org

Magnolia Farmers' Market
Saturday, 10am-2pm, June-October
Magnolia Community Center, 2550 34th Avenue W
www.seattlefarmersmarkets.org

Phinney Farmers' Market
Friday, 3pm-7pm, June-September
Phinney Neighborhood Center, 67th St and Phinney Ave N
www.seattlefarmersmarkets.org

Pike Place Market
All Week, 9am-6pm, All Year
Sundays, 10am-4pm, mid-June to October
Pike Place between Pike Street & Virginia Street
www.pikeplacemarket.org

Queen Anne Farmers' Market
Thursday, 3pm-7pm, June-September
Queen Anne Community Center
1st Ave N and Crockett St.
www.seattlemarkets.org

Tiny's Organic-Seattle Home Office
4660 East Marginal Way (East side of road) • Seattle • (206) 762-0577
www.tinysorganic.com

For years, Tiny's Organic has been known for their orchards in the Columbia
River Valley, where the weather conditions are ideal for growing stone fruit such as
peaches, plums, nectarines, and cherries. Tiny's Organics sells the fruit from their
own booths at over 30 weekly Farmers' Markets and recently expanded into selling
organic vegetables. For folks who now participate in their Community-Supported
Agriculture program, Tiny's delivers a large bag of farm-fresh organic fruit and vegetables to a Farmers' Market or convenient neighborhood drop in over 50 locations
throughout western Washington and the Olympic Peninsula. Pickup day is always
Wednesday for 22 weeks starting in June. See website for booth locations and drop-
off points.

University District Farmers' Market
Saturday, 9am-2pm, All Year
NE 50th Street & University Way NE
www.seattlefarmersmarkets.org

Wallingford Farmers' Market
Wednesday, 3pm-7pm, May-September
North 45th and Wallingford Ave
www.seattlemarkets.org

West Seattle Farmers' Market
Sunday, 10am-2pm, April-December
California Avenue SW & SW Alaska
www.seattlefarmersmarkets.org

SHORELINE

Taco Del Mar
1291 N 205th St • Shoreline • (206) 533-8226 • www.tacodelmar.com
See review – Seattle

Central Market Shoreline
15505 Westminster Way N • Shoreline • (206) 363-9226
www.shoreline.central-market.com

A major market that consciously caters to all dietary lifestyles: vegan, vegetarian, allergies, macrobiotic and conventional. The produce department comprises 20% of the store and offers a huge selection of organic along with local, Asian, and conventional produce. The bulk foods area has over 500 different items. Full line of dietary supplements, herbs, tea, and natural body care including a large selection of bulk bar soaps. Open daily 7am-11pm.

SNOHOMISH

Snohomish Farmers' Market
Thursday, 3pm-8pm, May-September
Carnegie Parking Lot, Cedar between 1st and Pearl Street
www.snohomishmarkets.com

SNOQUALMIE

Taco Del Mar
7802 Center Blvd SE • Snoqualmie Ridge • (425) 396-0465
www.tacodelmar.com
See review – Seattle

Snoqualmie Farmers' Market
Saturday, 10am-2pm, June-September
Maple and SR 202
www.snoqualmiefarmersmarket.com

SUMNER

Taco Del Mar
15127 Main St • Sumner • (253) 891-0209 • www.tacodelmar.com
See review – Seattle

TACOMA

DINING

East & West Café
5319 Tacoma Mall Blvd • Tacoma • (253) 475-7755
2514 N Proctor • Tacoma • (253) 756-5092

VegFriendly • PanAsian • Daily lunch & dinner • Full service & take out
Entrées $9-12

An elegant restaurant that prides itself on its fresh, local produce, high standards
with no MSG, and healthy flavorful cooking. Mostly Thai and Vietnamese cuisine,
along with a few Indian, Korean, Malaysian, and Indonesian dishes are offered with
a variety of vegetarian dishes like curries, soups, and salads. Non-vegetarian dishes
can be customized as completely vegetarian or vegan. Customers are encouraged to
order dishes they prefer and which may not be on the menu.

Quickie Too
1324 Martin Luther King Ave S • Tacoma • (253) 572-4549

Vegan-organic • Sandwich shop • Daily lunch • Mon, Wed, Fri dinner

Intentionally low-key but notably high-profile sandwiches made from home-made
seitan, tempeh or tofu. Raves for their Crazy Jamaican Burger which is grilled plantain, onions, and tofu. Famous is their Macaroni & Yease, and the seitan "steak,"
mashed potatoes and vegan gravy. A brunch suggested is the polenta and vegan
French toast. The foods created and offered by this African-American family go on
and on. See the Seattle listing for the Hillside Quickie.

Taco Del Mar
12821 Pacific Ave S • Tacoma • (253) 539-3800 • www.tacodelmar.com
1908 Pacific Ave • Tacoma • (253) 572-8393
5738 N 26th St • Tacoma • (253) 761-7425
See review – Seattle

Wendy's Vietnamese Restaurant
430 East 25th St • Tacoma • (253) 572-4678

VegFriendly • Vietnamese • Daily lunch & early dinner • Entrées $5-10

In the food court of Freight House Square. Same great taste but a smaller version of Wendy's II.

Wendy's II Vietnamese Restaurant
5015 Tacoma Mall Blvd • Tacoma • (253) 471-0228

VegFriendly • Vietnamese • Daily lunch & dinner • Entrées $5-10

A great choice for vegetarian and vegan cuisine in Tacoma. Winner of several awards, including 3 stars, Tacoma News Tribune winner of the 1994 Golden Fork Award. The food is tasty as well as healthy, with no MSG used. Try the Tofu Salad Roll, the Sai Dai Tofu, or the Black Bean Tofu with Vegetables.

SHOPPING

Marlene's Market & Deli
2951 S 38th St • Tacoma • (253) 472-4080 • www.marlenesmarket-deli.com

Conveniently close to I-5 with all the best natural products available, including faux meats, organic produce, vegetarian foods, groceries, herbs, vitamins and supplements, and a wide selection of smoothies and wheat-grass beverages. The deli offers customers a sit-down area in a comfortable atmosphere within the store. In addition to soups and salads, the deli offers tasty plates of pasta and sandwiches such as their vegan Field Roast, Avocado Delight, and vegan bologna. There is a pleasant table area for a relaxed before or after shopping meal. Open Mon-Fri 9am-8pm, Sat 9am-7pm, Sun 11am-6pm.

Metropolitan Market
2420 N Proctor St • Tacoma • (253) 761-3663

A large, beautiful, upscale market with a great selection of vegan and vegetarian products. You'll find a salad bar, bulk bins, meat and cheese analogs, nut butters, baby foods, and frozen vegan and vegetarian foods as well as health and beauty aids and organics. Also has a deli with prepared foods like pasta, soups, and salads. Open 24 hrs daily.

FROM THE FARM

Proctor Farmers' Market
Saturday, 9am-2pm, April-October
N 27th Street at Proctor
www.proctorfarmersmarket.com

Tacoma Dome District Farmers' Market
Tuesday, 3pm-7pm, June-August
E 25th Street between D & G Streets
www.tacomafarmersmarket.com

Tacoma Farmers' Market
Thursday, 9am-2pm, May-October
Broadway between 9th & 11th

TUKWILA

Bai Tong
16876 South Center Parkway • Tukwila • (206) 575-3366
See review – Seatac

California Pizza Kitchen
150 Andover Park W • Tukwila • Opening Soon
See review – Bellevue

Taco Del Mar
17410 Southcenter Pkwy • Tukwila • (206) 575-8587 • www.tacodelmar.com
See review – Seattle

Zoopa
Strander Blvd at Southcenter Plaza • Tukwila • (206) 575-0500 • www.zoopa.com

VeryVegFriendly • American Buffet • Daily lunch & dinner • Eat in or take-out
Special kids menu & high chairs

Fresh and healthy food in a convenient all you care to eat buffet format. Most items are vegetarian and there are many vegan items available. Many items such as prepared salads, dressings and soups are labeled vegetarian, low-fat, or fat-free. Vegans may want to check out the web site for specific information on soups and bakery ingredients. The website also offers special features, nutritional information, discounts, catering menus, and offers. The dining rooms are large and cheery with servers to help clear dishes making this an excellent choice for informal parties and large family gatherings.

UNIVERSITY PLACE

DINING

Taco Del Mar
2700 Bridgeport Way W • University Place • (253) 566-0555
www.tacodelmar.com
See review – Seattle

SHOPPING

Trader Joe's
3800 Bridgeport Way W • University Place • (253) 460-2672
See review – Seattle

Whole Foods Market
6810 27th St W • University Place • (253) 565-0188
See review – Seattle·

WOODINVILLE

Taco Del Mar
13780 NE 175th Ave NE • Woodinville • (425) 398-8183 • www.tacodelmar.com
See review – Seattle

Woodinville Farmers' Market
Saturday, 9am-3pm, May-October • Woodinville Village
Hwy 202 and Woodinville-Redmond Rd
www.woodinvillefarmersmarket.com

Seattle/Tacoma

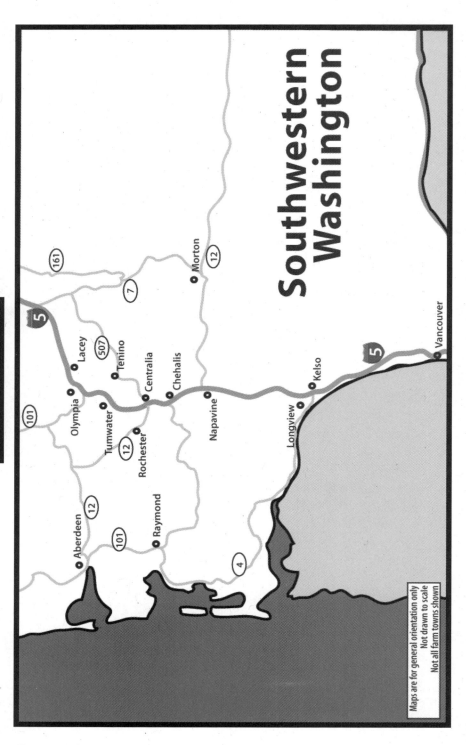

Southwestern Washington

Aberdeen

Olympia
Lacey
Tumwater
Tenino
Rochester
Raymond
Centralia
Chehalis
Napavine
Morton
Longview
Kelso
Vancouver

101
12
161
507
7
12
12
101
4
12
5
5

Maps are for general orientation only
Not drawn to scale
Not all farm towns shown

Southwestern Washington

ABERDEEN

Thai Carrot
412 S Boone St • Aberdeen • (360) 532-2044

VegFriendly • Thai • Tues-Sat lunch & dinner • Sun dinner only • Closed Mon

The Thai Carrot, while not a vegan/vegetarian restaurant, does have many menu choices that are easily adaptable. Most items come with a choice of vegetable, tofu, or meat options. The curries, for example, are not made with fish sauce, and they are incredible! They are very happy to discuss which menu items are suitable. All food is made fresh on the premises.

The Market Place
822 E Wishkah St • Aberdeen • (360) 538-1521

Antique and contemporary fixtures greet the eye in this clean, neat, well-lit store. The focus on health includes top-quality supplements and personal-care products. An extensive bulk food, herb, and spice section is available as well as conveniently packaged foods, refrigerated and freezer items, and a large low-carb section. Open Mon-Fri 9:30am-5:30pm, Sat 9:30am-5pm.

BATTLE GROUND

Old Town Saturday Market
Saturday, 9am-3pm, April-October
SE 2nd Ave & East Main
www.otbgsm.com

BRUSH PRAIRIE

Hunters' Greens Farm
11116 NE 156th Street • Brush Prairie • (360) 256-3788
www.huntersgreens.com

A Community-Supported-Agriculture family farm since 2001, Hunters' Greens offers organic vegetables for the 24-week season, June through mid-November. Flower shares are available.

CENTRALIA

DINING

Berry Fields
201 S Pearl • Centralia • (360) 736-1183

VegFriendly • American • Breakfast & lunch • Full service & take out • Entrées $5-10

Black-bean veggie burgers are great. Ask for meatless stir-fry. They bake and sell their own oat bread. Friendly, efficient service.

Panda Inn
806 Harrison Ave • Centralia • (360) 807-2088

VegFriendly • Chinese • Daily lunch & dinner • Entrées $5-10

Vegetarian dishes in each category of Chinese food. Will substitute tofu for meat in many dishes. Large, pleasant room with many tables.

SHOPPING

Good Health Nutrition Center
503 Harrison Avenue • Centralia • (360) 736-3830

The Good Health Nutrition Center is an important resource for the greater Centralia region. Vegetarians will find everything they need at this store. Everything from meat substitutes to tofu and tempeh is available. Also featured is a good selection of organic produce and bulk bins. Rounding out their stock is an excellent selection of supplements and health and beauty aids. A sandwich shop is located in the rear of the store where a vegetarian can get a good lunch while shopping. Parking is very convenient and the staff is quite knowledgeable. Open Mon-Sat 9am-6pm.

FROM THE FARM

Lewis County Farmers' Market
Friday, 9am-3pm, May-September
Pine & Tower

CHEHALIS

DINING

Aldente
545 N Market Blvd • Chehalis • (360) 740-8000

VegFriendly • Italian • Tue-Sat lunch & dinner • Entrées around $10

Rich and wonderful food. All the pasta dishes on the menu are vegetarian and the chef is very willing to accommodate vegans. Friendly, helpful, and efficient service.

Market Street Bakery & Café

492 N Market • Chehalis • (360) 748-0875

VegFriendly • Eclectic • Snacks & lunch • Daily 8:30am-5pm • Full service & take out • Entrées under $5

The wonderful, freshly baked breads are their highlight. All soups (except clam chowder) are veggie.

Plaza Jalisco

1340 NW Maryland • Chehalis • (360) 748-4298

VegFriendly • Mexican • Daily lunch & dinner • Full service & take out • Entrées $5-10

Small and crowded, but the food is so delicious that many local people go there. Waiters are efficient and friendly. They have recently added a veggie selection to the menu, including vegetarian enchiladas, burritos, and fajitas. Moving into a newly renovated building at the same location shortly, they're sure to serve the same delicious food to lots more people.

Taco Del Mar

1435 NW Louisiana Ave • Chehalis • (360) 767 0800
See review – Seattle

FROM THE FARM

Community Farmers' Market

Tuesday, Noon-4pm, June-October
Boistfort Square between Market Boulevard and Pacific Ave
www.lewis.wsu.edu/family/cfm.html

CURTIS

Boistfort Valley Farm

426 Boistfort Road • Curtis • (360) 245-3796 • www.BoistfortValleyFarm.com

Each week since 1994, Boistfort Valley Farm Community-Supported-Agriculture members have received a box full of fresh certified-organic produce, including a selection from their herb garden, a bouquet of cut flowers, recipes, and serving suggestions. June through October.

HOCKINSON

Purple Rain Vineyard

21313 NE 147th Street • Hockinson • (360) 256-8658
www.purplerainvineyard.com

Offering "Authentic Food/Beyond Organic" from their "potage garden" since 1989, Purple Rain Vineyard harvests vegetables, small fruit, and culinary and medicinal herbs. Flower shares are available. 22-week Community-Supported-Agriculture farm, May to October, with pickup at the farm.

ILWACO

Saturday Market at The Port of Ilwaco
Saturday, 10am-4pm, May-September
Waterfront Way

KELSO

Plaza Jalisco
400 West Main • Kelso • (360) 425-7476
See review – Chehalis

Kelso Bridge Market
Sunday, 10am-3pm, May-September
Allen Street & Pacific Avenue under the Allen Street Bridge
www.kelso.gov/recreation/bridgemarket

LACEY

Emperor's Palace
7321 Martin Way SE • Lacey • (360) 923-2323
See review – Olympia

Taco Del Mar
730 Sleater-Kinney Rd SE • Lacey • (360) 491-9564 • www.tacodelmar.com
1350 Marvin Road NE • Lacey • (360) 456-8120
See review – Seattle

LONGVIEW

Cowlitz County Community Farmers' Market
Tuesday-9am-2pm, April-October
Cowlitz County Fairgrounds at 7th & New York

Wednesday, Noon-5pm, May-September
Downtown on Broadway and Commerce

Saturday, 9am-2pm, April-October
Cowlitz County Fairgrounds at 7th & New York
www.cowlitzfarmersmarket.com

MORTON

Plaza Jalisco
200 Westlake Ave • Morton • (360) 496-6660
See review – Chehalis

NAPAVINE

Plaza Jalisco
120 Birch St SW • Napavine • (360) 262-0243
See review – Chehalis

OLYMPIA

DINING

Emperor's Palace
400 Cooper Point Rd SW • Olympia • (360) 754-2188 • www.eprestaurant.com

VeryVegFriendly • Chinese • Daily lunch & dinner • Entrées $5-10

Vegetarian food delivered! A separate vegetarian menu of about 30 items offers tasty, traditional Chinese fare like hot and spicy Ma Po's Tofu, with diced tofu stir-fried with peppers, onions, and tomatoes in a rich, spicy brown sauce. The hot-and-sour soup is a treat, and vegan. The Broccoli and Mushroom with Ginger Sauce has just the right amount of zip. The Cashew Vegetables are extremely rich and flavorful, swiming in cashews and sauce. Emperor's Palace is a great excuse to put your feet up at home, and call your meal in.

Great Cuisine of India
116 4th Ave W • Olympia • (360) 943-3442

VegFriendly • Indian • Daily lunch buffet and dinner • Entrées $5-15

Specializing in northern Indian cuisine, this classic Indian restaurant serves up plenty of vegetarian choices.

The Lemon Grass Restaurant
212 4th Ave W • Olympia • (360) 705-1832

VegFriendly • Thai & Asian • Daily lunch & dinner • Closed Sun • Full service • Entrées $5-10

Beautiful, flavorful food, fresh, hot, and perfectly spiced. Innovative ingredients make the food fun and interesting, like the Purple Passion, made with Asian eggplant, jicama, green beans, tofu, basil, and a yellow-bean and garlic sauce. The vegetarian items do not contain fish sauce like most Thai restaurants, so rest easy. Go with a friend and split one of the many exotic choices such as Lemon Grass Garden, Swimming Angel or Jungle Prince.

Le Voyeur

404 East 4th Ave • Olympia • (360) 943-5710

Vegetarian • Eclectic • Daily lunch & dinner • Full service • Entrées $5-10

Get ready for the best vegetarian home cookin' within a 100 mile radius! Try an open-faced tofu sandwich with mushroom gravy, the Sloppy Hippie with tempeh and grilled onions, or chicken-fried tofu with home fries. Their salad dressings and gravies are masterpieces. The décor is funky and extremely casual. For entertainment, wear your Birkenstocks, hang out with the 20-somethings, watch the cooks (the kitchen is almost part of the dining room), drink your water out of Ball canning jars, and go to the little lounge in back and listen to local bands. Extensive, reasonably priced wine list.

Saigon Rendezvous

117 West 5th Ave • Olympia • (360) 352-1989

VeryVegFriendly • Chinese & Vietnamese • Daily lunch & dinner • Full service
Entrées $5-10

A huge vegan menu with over 75 choices makes this vegetarian heaven. Soy-based "meat" imitations are a specialty here; with items like "Prawns" with Lemon Grass, BBQ "Pork," and Kung Pao "Chicken." Tofu is also plentiful. Try the Tofu with Peapods—the colors are beautiful and the flavors great. The large appetizer platter is amazing, with five types of hors d'oeuvres, served at the table with a flaming mini-caldron to cook the skewers of Teriyaki "Beef." With great food, lots of choices, and friendly service, it's a real find.

SHOPPING

Olympia Food Co-op

3111 Pacific Ave SE • Olympia • (360) 956-3870
921 N Rogers • Olympia • (360) 754-7666

This co-op features a grab-and-go deli, with six different menu rotations and several vegetarian and vegan options, including Cilantro Pesto Pasta, Smoked Tofu Sandwich, Curried Tempeh, and Nori Rolls. Organic foods are used whenever possible. The Olympia Food Co-op is a member-owned, collectively run natural-food grocery store with two locations. Extensive volunteer working-member program. Support for local farmers and local production. Organic foods and fresh organic produce, bulk and deli items available. Daily 9am-9pm.

FROM THE FARM

Olympia Farmers' Market

Thursday-Sunday, 10am-3pm, April-December
Saturday & Sunday only November & December
Capitol Way & Market Street
www.olympiafarmersmarket.com

RAYMOND

Public Market on the Willapa
Friday & Saturday, 10am-5pm, May to mid-December
4th & Heath

ROCHESTER

Helsing Junction Farm
12013 Independence Road • (360) 273-2033 • www.helsingfarmcsa.com

For sixteen years, Helsing-Junction Community-Supported Agriculture members have received a pre-packed box of seasonal vegetables, fruits, and flowers, all grown organically. Weekly shares are brought to convenient pick-up locations in Seattle, Olympia, Tacoma, and Portland. One bunch of flowers as well as a weekly newsletter and a page of gourmet recipes are included in each share, large or small. Helsing Junction works hard at cultivating a personal relationship with CSA members, many of whom have been with them for the entire 16 years.

Rising River Farm
13208 201 Ave SW • 360-273-5368 • www.risingriverfarm.com

Since 1994, quality, organic vegetables and herbs have been grown for Community-Supported Agriculture members. On-farm sales and at the Olympia Farmers' Market.

TENINO

Tenino Farmers' Market
Saturday, 10am-3pm, June-September
Old Highway 99 and Garfield Ave E
www.teninofarmersmarket.org

TUMWATER

DINING

Plaza Jalisco
5212 Capital Blvd • Tumwater • (360) 709-0287
See review – Chehalis

Taco Del Mar
555 Trosper Rd SW • Tumwater • (360) 753-6100 • www.tacodelmar.com
See review – Seattle

FROM THE FARM

Tumwater Town Center Farmers' Market
Wednesday, 11am-2pm, May-October
SW corner of Capitol Blvd and Israel Rd
www.tumwaterfarmersmarket.org

VANCOUVER

DINING

Bamboo Hut
800 NE Tenney Road (in the Fred Meyer shopping center) • Vancouver • (360) 574-1351

VeryVegFriendly • Pan-Asian • Daily lunch and dinner

The Bamboo Hut features Asian cuisine with an emphasis on Japanese specialties. Try the Teriyaki Soy Chicken and the Tofu Yakisoba. Look for daily specials. Vegetable appetizers and brown rice round out the healthy offerings at this most special restaurant. Service is good and there is plenty of free parking.

Casa Grande
2014 Main St • Vancouver • (360) 694-7031 • www.casagranderestaurant.com

VegFriendly • Mexican • Daily lunch & dinner • Full service

Casa Grande, located in a grand, remodeled house on Main Street, offers traditional Mexican cuisine. There are lots of vegetarian options available, although they do emphasize dairy. Some vegan options are available by request. Try the Squash Enchiladas or the Veggie Burrito (vegans can hold the cheese). This restaurant proclaims itself a trans-fat-free zone. Some out door seating is available in the warmer seasons.

Sweet Tomatoes
12601 SE 2nd Circle • Vancouver • 360-891-0240 • www.sweettomatoes.com

VegFriendly • Salad bar • Daily lunch & dinner • Sunday brunch

Sweet Tomatoes is a family-friendly, self-serve, salad-buffet restaurant offering much more than just salad. All items have very clearly marked ingredients and there are many vegetarian and vegan options. You can go back for seconds, so bring an appetite. The atmosphere is light and cheerful. Take out is available. The staff is helpful and parking is very convenient.

Taco Del Mar

8902 NE 5th Ave • Vancouver • (360) 576-6375 • www.tacodelmar.com
19111 SE 34th St • Vancouver • (360) 885-1030
221G NE 104th • Vancouver • (360) 883-2400
700 Washington St • Vancouver • (360) 693-7065
11211 NE 4th Plain • Vancouver • Opening soon
See review – Seattle

SHOPPING

Trader Joe's

305 SE Chkalov St • Vancouver • (360) 883-9000 • www.traderjoes.com
See description – Seattle

Wild Oats Natural Marketplace

815 SE 160th Ave • Vancouver • (360) 253-4082 • www.wildoats.com

Now part of the Whole Foods chain of stores, Wild Oats is an attractive store offering a wide range of natural and organic foods, recycled paper products, fresh flowers, unique gift items, and a large selection of supplements and body care items. There is a full-service deli with vegetarian and vegan offerings. The new store is considerably larger, providing more space for more products, the ability to bring in newer products for showcase, better organization and more space for shopping. Open daily 8am-10pm.

FROM THE FARM

Hidden Oasis Farm

5410 NE 229th Court • Vancouver • (360) 256-6896

Hidden Oasis uses only the manual and heirloom methods of farming of our ancestors to promote the health of the soil and thus the health of the produce and plants that are grown in that soil. The farm produces vegetables, herbs, shiitake mushrooms, Asian pears, blackberries, apples, plums, and flowers. There is pick-up at the farm and delivery to Vancouver locations from April to mid-October. Winter shares of limited products are also available.

Storytree Farm

6227 NE 124th Street • Vancouver • (360) 576-7139
www.StorytreeFarm.com

This farm grows vegetables, herbs, greens, and gourmet lettuces using sustainable practices and without the use of pesticides or herbicides. Also available are flowers, honey, grapes, figs, apples, Shiro plums, melons, and heirloom pumpkins. Pick up food at the farm. Twenty weeks, June thru October.

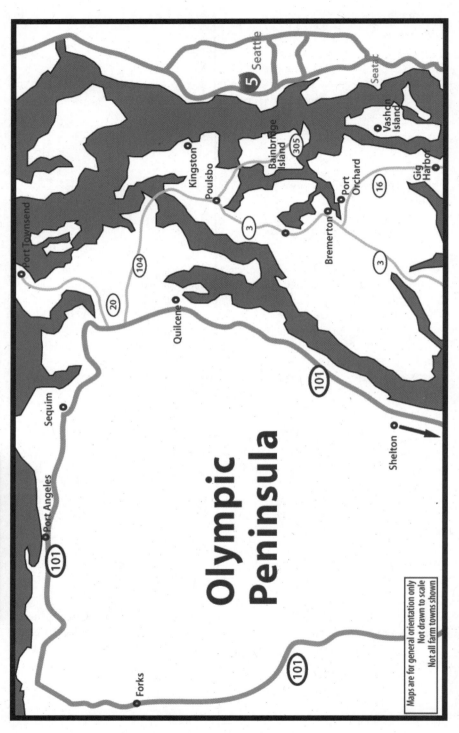

Olympic Peninsula

Maps are for general orientation only
Not drawn to scale
Not all farm towns shown

72

Olympic Peninsula

BAINBRIDGE ISLAND

DINING

Emmy's Vege House
100 Winslow Way W • Bainbridge Island • (206) 855-2996

Vegan • Vietnamese • Mon-Sat lunch & dinner • Closed Sun • Take-out only
Entrees $5-$7

This small take-out restaurant has eight outdoor (covered) tables where you can enjoy your food if you don't wish to take it home. 100-percent vegetable- and soy-protein meat substitutes are used, with dishes such as Kabob, Noodle Salad, Golden Tofu, and Braised Eggplant.

Sawatdy Thai Cuisine
8770 Fletcher Bay Road • Bainbridge Island • (206) 780-2429

VegFriendly • Thai • Lunch Tue-Fri • Dinner Tue-Sun • Closed Mon
Full service, take-out • Entrées $5-10

This elegant Thai restaurant is rated as one of the best restaurants on Bainbridge Island and is listed in several Best Places guides. It serves a wide variety of Thai and South East Asian dishes, with many vegetarian options. You can also request any meat-based dish be served with tofu replacing the meat. Special sunken table for large parties at the end of the room. Make reservations.

FROM THE FARM

Bainbridge Island Farmers' Markets
Wednesday, 4pm-7pm, July-September
Saturday, 9am-1pm, April-October
Market Square 208 Madison & Winslow Way

Saturday, 10am-3pm, November-December
Eagle Harbor Church, 105 Winslow Way & Madison
www.bainbridgefarmersmarket.com

BREMERTON

Taco Del Mar
7058 State Hwy 303 NE • Bremerton • (360) 307-8226 • www.tacodelmar.com
100 Washington Ave • Bremerton • (360) 782-2505
See review – Seattle

FORKS

Plaza Jalisco
90 Forks Ave • Forks • (360) 374-3108
See review – Chehalis

GIG HARBOR

Taco Del Mar
5500 Olympic Dr • Gig Harbor • (253) 857-7807
See review – Seattle

Gig Harbor Farmers' Market
Saturday, 8:30am-2pm, April-September
3500 Hunt Street NW at Hwy 16
www.gigharborfarmersmarket.com

KINGSTON

Kingston Farmers' Market
Saturday, 9am-2:30pm, April-October
Port of Kingston Marina Park
www.kingstonfarmersmarket.com

PORT ANGELES

DINING

Café Garden
1506 E 1st St • Port Angeles • (360) 457-4611

VegFriendly • American • Daily breakfast & lunch • Thur-Mon Dinner

Start the day with pancakes or veggie omelets and scrambles. Creative salads and pasta dishes are the vegetarian choices offered for other meals.

Thai Peppers Restaurant
222 N Lincoln St • Port Angeles • (360) 452-4995

VegFriendly • Thai • Daily lunch & dinner • Closed Sun
Full service & take out

One block from the Victoria ferry, the friendly staff will guide you through the 20-plus vegetarian items such as tofu curries and stir-fried veggies, all with those enticing Thai flavors.

SHOPPING

Country Air Natural Foods Store
117 E First St • Port Angeles • (360) 452-7175

Fresh produce, packaged foods, bulk bins, and refrigerated items such as tofu and tempeh are all available at this natural-food store. They also have a juice bar, and you can order sandwiches, some of which may be vegetarian, from the restaurant downstairs. Open Mon-Sat 9am-6pm, Sun 11am-4pm.

Good to Go! Natural Grocery
1105 S Eunice St • Port Angeles • 360) 457 1857

An all-vegetarian grab-and-go food store featuring organic produce, fresh wraps, and sandwiches including hummus, tofu pate, and fresh salad ingredients, plus some soups and smoothies. Open Mon-Fri 8am-6pm, Sat 10am-5pm. Closed Sun.

FROM THE FARM

Farmers' Market of Clallam County
Saturday, 9am-3pm, March-December
1st & Washington

Port Angeles Farmers' Market
Saturday, 10am-2pm, All Year
Courthouse Parking Lot, 4th and Peabody Streets

Wednesday 3pm-6:30pm, June-October
Vincent Parking Lot 1st and Laurel
www.pafarmersmarket.net

Salt Creek Farm
310 Salt Creek Rd • Port Angeles • (360) 928-3583

Certified organic since 1993, Salt Creek's Community-Supported Agriculture program offers full- or half-share programs, in which heirloom produce is delivered once a week throughout the growing season. The land is planted to provide for a balanced harvest each week. Most of the items are picked right from the fields the same day they are delivered. Farm visits are encouraged, with children particularly welcomed.

PORT ORCHARD

Port Orchard Farmers' Market
Saturday, 9am-3pm, April-October
Harrison and Bay Street
www.pofarmersmarket.org

DINING

The Food Co-op Kitchen & Juice Bar
414 Kearney • Port Townsend • (360) 385-2883

VegFriendly • Deli & juice bar • Daily breakfast & lunch • Entrées $5-10

In 2001, this small co-op was elevated to a large store with many additional goods and services. A full-service deli was introduced which features freshly made organic salads and live foods as well as daily hot foods and soups. Additionally there is a wonderful juice bar. If you really want to "go native" this is the most vegetarian- and vegan-friendly place in town, and organic is standard here. It is where local artists, construction crews, earth mothers, wooden-boat sailors, and massage therapists all meet to eat. The "live" palak paneer is expensive but quite nice, as is the raw food pizza. There is a small area for sit down snacking inside the store.

Fountain Café
920 Washington St • Port Townsend • (360) 385-1364

Veg Friendly • Northwest eclectic • Daily lunch & dinner • Entrées $10-20

This cozy, casually elegant little place is well worth visiting one block off the beaten tourist path. The vegetarian biscuits and gravy are the best you are likely to find anywhere; large homemade biscuits served with a generous amount of fennel and wild mushroom gravy. For a fine lunch or dinner try a black bean burger or Portobello mushroom burger. The seafood crepes are excellent ordered with no seafood but extra mushrooms and spinach. You really can't go wrong here, though it is a much easier place to be vegetarian than vegan. Excellent wine list and service is always good.

Khu Larb Thai
225 Adams St • Port Townsend • (360) 385-5023

VeryVegFriendly • Thai • Daily lunch & dinner • Closed Mon • Full service & take out • Entrées $5-10

Everything that a Thai restaurant should be, pleasing vegetarians, vegans, and meat-and-fish eaters at the same table. There is a vegetarian entrée for every letter of the alphabet. The signature spices are used in generous, well-balanced amounts. Vegetarian Tom Kha soup is as hearty as it is tasty, with lots of vegetables and tofu, a meal in itself. Classic Phud Thai without egg stands as a vegan treat. Curries are all delicious and the Spicy Eggplant is not to be missed. Lovely, thoughtful ambiance, unobtrusively good service, and live jazz vibraphone on the weekends.

The Land Fall
412 Waterfront St • Port Townsend • (360) 385-5814

VegFriendly • Eclectic • Daily breakfast & lunch • Full service or take out
Entrées $5-10

Olympic Peninsula

Peculiar architecture, funky atmosphere, and great location overlooking the Point Hudson Yacht Harbor make it a favorite of locals and boaters for casual dining. It serves delicious confetti coleslaw and has backyard picnic tables for warmer days. There is a special vegetarian penalty. If you don't want to eat hamburger for lunch, expect to pay $1.50 extra for a veggie burger! The veggie quesadillas are the best vegetarian item on the menu.

Lehanis Deli & Coffee House
221 Taylor St • Port Townsend • (360) 385-3961

VeryVegFriendly • Deli & coffee house • Daily breakfast & lunch • Cafeteria or take out • Entrées $5-10

A very pleasant little coffee house which is both vegetarian- and vegan-friendly. You can get a delicious organic soymilk latte and some really nice soups, and treats and snacks in both vegan and vegetarian choices mostly from local organic produce. Vegan chocoholics can indulge here. They now offer gluten and/or wheat free baked goods and meals.

Hudson Point Café
130 Hudson St • Port Townsend • (360) 379-0592

Veg Friendly • Creative family style • Tues-Sat breakfast, lunch & dinner • Sun brunch • Closed Mon • Full service or take out • Entrées $5-10

On the far point, across the yacht harbor from town, in one of the historical old white Point Hudson buildings with a fine view of the small harbor (yes, otters do live under them and raid the boats of incautious yachtsmen). At this charming, out-of-the-way place, you can get a vegan breakfast of oatmeal with soymilk, and there are plenty of veggie choices including soups, salads, sandwiches, and pasta. Classic Port Townsend nautical ambience with an ever-changing water view and breakfast all day.

The Salal Café
634 Waterfront St • Port Townsend • (360) 385-6532

VegFriendly • Northwest eclectic • Daily breakfast & lunch • Full service & take out • Entrées $5-10

A long-standing commitment to vegetarian dining, with options such as tofu scramble for breakfast, tofu stir-fry, and a Tofu Rueben sandwich for lunch. Overall, it's a fine place to eat with good service and a pleasant sunny atmosphere in an old building right on the main tourist drag.

Sweet Laurette & Cyndee's Café & Patisserie
1029 Lawrence St • Port Townsend • (360) 385-4886

VegFriendly • Bakery & Northwest eclectic • Daily breakfast & lunch, Sun brunch Closed Tues • Full service or take out • Entrées $5-10

The food is creative and trendy. For lunch, have a delicious, grilled-vegetable Panini, the vegatini sandwich, the vegan delight, or a large salad served with a choice of several soups, at least one of which is vegan. Any meal with meat will be served without for $1 off. They have excellent expresso, served almost too beautifully to drink, and great chai as well. French toast fans may just find Sweet Laurette's Stuffed French Toast to be the best.

FROM THE FARM

Colinwood Farms
1210 F St • Port Townsend • (360) 379-9610

A summer Community-Supported Agriculture and winter produce program. All produce is 100% organic.

Jefferson County Farmers' Markets
Wednesday, 3:30pm-6:30pm, June-September
Uptown on Polk and Lawrence

Saturday, 9:30am-1:30pm, May-November
Uptown on Tyler and Lawrence
www.ptfarmersmarket.org

POULSBO

DINING

Taco Del Mar
21555 Olhava Way NW (College Market Place) • Poulsbo • (360) 598-2501
www.tacodelmar.com
See review – Seattle

SHOPPING

Central Market
20148 10th Ave E • Poulsbo • (206) 522-4588 • www.central-market.com

A major market which consciously caters to all dietary lifestyles: vegan, vegetarian, allergies, macrobiotic, and conventional. The produce department comprises 20% of the store and offers a huge selection of organic along with local, Asian, and conventional produce. The bulk foods area has over 500 different items. The natural resources department has a full line of dietary supplements, herbs, tea, and natural body care including a large selection of bulk bar soaps. The natural foods/organics department has become so popular that they have expanded. This means the number of items and variety of items has substantially increased. Open 24 hrs daily.

FROM THE FARM

Poulsbo Farmers' Market
Saturday, 9am-1pm, April-October
Poulsbo Village Medical/Dental Center, 7th Avenue & Iverson
www.poulsbofarmersmarket.org

QUILCENE

Quilcene Farmers' Marketplace
Saturday, 9am-3pm, April-September
Hwy 101 and Center Ave

SEQUIM

Sunny Farms Country Store
261461 Highway 101 • Sequim • (360) 683-8003

A natural food store selling fresh produce, packaged and refrigerated items, and bulk foods. The deli has some vegetarian items, and coffee is available. Open daily 8am-8pm.

SHELTON

Shelton Farmers' Market
Saturday, 9am-2pm, May-September
3rd Street between Cedar & Franklin
www.sheltonfarmersmarket.com

SILVERDALE

Taco Del Mar
2244 NW Bucklin Hill Rd • Silverdale • (360) 307-8226 • www.tacodelmar.com
See review – Seattle

Peninsula Farmers' Market
Tuesday, 11am-4pm, April-September
Silverdale Beach Hotel (Bucklin Hill Road)

Olympic Peninsula

VASHON ISLAND

DINING

Homegrown Café
17614 Vashon Hwy • Vashon Island • (206) 463-6302

VegFriendly • Café • Breakfast and lunch only, closes at 3pm

Natural home-style cooking with a flair. Many vegetarian and vegan choices like Mediterranean Pasta with Artichokes or Brown Rice and Lentil Curry. The home-made Boogle Burger is highly recommended, as is the Tofu Scramble.

SHOPPING

Minglement
19529 Vashon Hwy SW • Vashon Island • (206) 463 9672

A great little natural food store in the heart of Vashon, offering organic produce, bulk products, refrigerated and frozen items, and snack items. They now offer state-licensed raw milk, a coffee roastery, and herbs and supplements as well. Open Mon-Fri 7am-5pm, Sat 8am-4pm and Sun 10am-3pm.

FROM THE FARM

Vashon Farmers' Market
Wednesday, 3pm-6pm, July-September
Saturday, 10am-2pm, April-October
Vashon Hwy & Bank Road
www.vigavashon.org

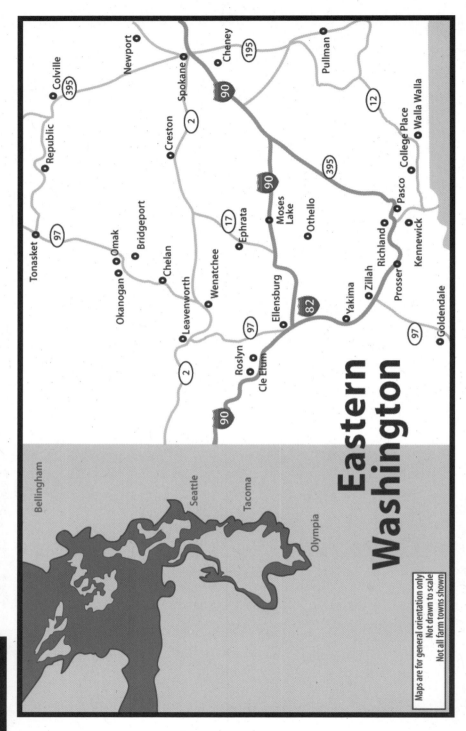

Eastern Washington

Maps are for general orientation only
Not drawn to scale
Not all farm towns shown

Eastern Washington

BRIDGEPORT

Bridgeport Farmers' Market
Friday, 8:30am-12:30pm, June to mid-October

CHELAN

Bear Foods Market
125 E Woodin Avenue • Chelan • (509) 682-5535 • www.bearfoods.com

Bear Foods Market carries a broad selection of natural groceries, produce, bulk foods, herbs & spices, botanicals, vitamins & supplements, and health & beauty supplies, as well as other non-foods items. Both organic and non-organic foods are stocked. All products are selected for quality, taste and nutrition. They have extensive experience sourcing quality bulk foods from the best suppliers and they package many foods at their own facilities. The highest quality spices and culinary herbs available are offered. Store hours are Mon-Sat 9am-7pm (6pm in winter), Sun 11am-5pm. Golden Florins Café and Juice Bar is adjacent to Bear Foods Market, offering panini sandwiches, soup made fresh daily at the café, vegetable & fruit juices, and smoothies. It is open Mon-Sat 10am-4pm, closed Sundays.

Lake Chelan Valley Farmers' Market
Saturday, 8am-1pm, June-October
Johnson & Columbia in Chamber parking lot

CHENEY

Friday Farmers' Market
Friday, 11am-4:30pm, May-October
1st & College

CLE ELUM

Taco Del Mar
801 W Davis St • Cle Elum • (509) 674-6998
See review – Seattle

COLLEGE PLACE

DINING

His Garden & Bakery

28 SE 12th • College Place • (509) 525-1040

Vegetarian • Deli • Mon-Thurs dinner • Sun-Fri breakfast & lunch • Closed Sat

An excellent vegetarian deli where about half the choices are vegan. Soups, sandwiches, vegan cheese, and "Haystacks," burritos. Eat there or take home. The bakery makes lots of whole grain breads from fresh ground flour. Also offers a small store offering a selection of healthy vegetarian and vegan foods, bulk herbs, bakery, and deli items. Lots of fresh whole-grain breads baked on premises.

Walla Walla College Cafeteria

32 SE Ash • College Place • (509) 527-2732

Vegetarian • Cafeteria • Daily when class is in session • Limited hours in summer

Vegan eats are also available in this youthful setting where all the food is meat-free, including the make-your-own Mexican meal table. Soups, salads, and pastas, of course.

SHOPPING

Andy's Market

1117 S College Ave • College Place • (509) 529-1003 • www.andysmarket.com

A full service natural foods store, selling mostly vegetarian foods, including fresh produce, bulk grains, packaged foods, etc. Fresh sandwiches are available. Open Sun-Thurs 7am-9pm, Fri 7am-2hrs before sundown. Closed Sat.

COLVILLE

Mt. Sunflower Natural Market

358 N Main St • Colville • (509) 684-4211

A small store selling some packaged foods and bulk items. Fresh juice and smoothies and a staff ready answer your questions. Open Mon-Fri 9am-6pm, Sat 9am-5pm. Closed Sun.

Colville Farmers' Market

Wednesday, Noon-6pm, June-October
Corner of Oak Street & 3rd Avenue

Saturday, 8:30am-1pm, May-October
Corner of Main & Astor

CRESTON

Redwine Canyon Farm
37529 Redwine Canyon Rd • Creston • (509) 636-3366

A full-service Community-Supported Agriculture farm, Redwine Canyon offers fresh, naturally grown produce for communities from Coulee Dam to Spokane. Organic produce, cut flowers, nuts, and fruits are sold from the farm.

EAST WENATCHEE

Eastmont Farmers' Market
Wednesday and Saturday 8am-12pm, June-September
Friday, 3pm-6pm, June-September
Big R Parking Lot at 260 Highline and 2nd St SE

ELLENSBURG

DINING

Taco Del Mar
1614 Canyon Road • Ellensburg •(509) 962-3009
See review – Seattle

Valley Café
105 W 3rd • Ellensburg • (509) 925-3050

VegFriendly • Eclectic • Lunch & dinner daily • Entrées $5-10

You can eat well at this 1938 classic Art Deco bistro. Seven out of twelve entrées are cheese- and butter-rich vegetarian meals. A majority of the tasty appetizers and large salads are fully vegetarian. Pasta Primavera is a vegan entrée on offer and the chef is happy to make other dishes vegetarian or vegan upon request.

SHOPPING

Super 1 Foods
200 E Mt View Ave • Ellensburg • (509) 525-8790

Inside this regular grocery store is a special natural-foods department, sponsored by Huckleberry's Natural Market. They sell packaged foods, frozen and refrigerated vegetarian and vegan foods, and bulk items. The grocery store sells a wide range of fresh fruits and vegetables. Open 5am-1am.

FROM THE FARM

Kittitas County Farmers' Market
Saturday, 9am-1pm, May-October
4th Avenue between Pearl & Pine
www.kcfarmersmarket.com

EPHRATA

Ephrata Farmers' Market
Saturday, 8am-Noon, June-October
Sun Basin Plaza on Basin Street

GOLDENDALE

Goldendale Saturday Market
Saturday, 9am-2pm, May-October
Vern Markee Park at 903 E Broadway

KENNEWICK

DINING

Taco Del Mar
2632 W Kennewick Ave • Kennewick • (509) 735-1111
See review – Seattle

Toeshi Teriyaki & Korean
7935 W Granville Blvd • Kennewick • (509) 734-9339

VegFriendly • Korean • Lunch & dinner • Closed Sunday • Entrées $5-10

This is a family-owned-and-operated restaurant that is very authentic, and they happily accommodate vegetarians and vegans. Most items are prepared from scratch. Their kim chee and sautéed tofu is reported to be the best in the Tri-cities. Vegetable Fried Rice is a local favorite. Clean, relaxed, and family-friendly.

SHOPPING

Highland Healthfood Superstore
101 Vista Way • Kennewick • (509) 783-7147

A grocery store selling fresh produce, packaged foods, frozen vegetarian items, and bulk foods. Open Mon-Thurs 9:30am-8pm, Fri 9:30am-3pm, Sun 12pm-5pm. Closed Sat.

FROM THE FARM

Kennewick Farmers' Market
Thursday, 4pm-8pm, June-October
Kennewick Avenue & Auburn Street

LEAVENWORTH

Renaissance Café
217 8th St • Leavenworth • (509) 548-6725 • www.therenaissancecafe.com

VegFriendly • American • Daily breakfast & lunch • Thurs-Sat dinner • Full service
& take-out • Entrees $5-10

Just a block behind the main front street in Leavenworth, you can find a great
selection of vegetarian options at this cosy café. Get an early start with a breakfast
of tofu scramble or breakfast wrap with veggie sausage. For lunch, try the Bohemian
wrap or the Garden Veggie sandwich. Dinner is served Thursday through Saturdays—
don't miss the God Food (Linguini tossed with Special Garlic Soy Tahini sauce).

Wenatchee Valley Farmers' Market
Tuesday, 8am-1pm, June-October
Downtown on Front Street and Leavenworth
info@wenatcheefarmersmarket.com

MILLWOOD

Millwood Community Farmers' Market
Wednesday, 3pm-7pm, May-October
Millwood Presbyterian Church
Knox & Marguerite Street

MOSES LAKE

Taco Del Mar
2707 W Broadway • Moses Lake • Opening soon
See review – Seattle

NEWPORT

Pend Oreille Valley Farmers' Market
Saturday, 9am-1pm, May-October
3rd between Union and Washington

OKANOGAN

Okanogan Valley Farmers' Market
Saturday, 9am-1pm, May-October
American Legion Park

OMAK

Okanogan Valley Farmers' Market
Tuesday, 3pm-7pm, June-October
Civic League Park at Central & Ash Streets

OTHELLO

Othello Farmers' Market
Saturday, 8am-Noon, June to mid-October
Pioneer Park at 3rd & Main

PASCO

Pasco Farmers' Market
Wednesday & Saturday, 8am-12pm, May-October
4th & Columbia

PROSSER

Prosser Farmers' Market
Saturday, 8am-Noon, May-October
Prosser City Park at 7th Street & Sommer Avenue
www.prosserfarmersmarket.com

PULLMAN

Swilly's
200 NE Kamaken St • Pullman • (509) 334-3395 • www.swillys.com

VegFriendly • Eclectic • Mon-Fri lunch • Mon-Sat dinner • Closed Sun
Full service • Lunch $5-$10, Dinner $15-20

This upscale restaurant is one of the most popular in town. For lunch, choose from black-bean chili, a Mediterranean plate, a veggie burger, or pita sandwich. In the evening, the coconut vegetable curry or the Thai Shrimp Saute can be served with fresh tofu (instead of shrimp), or choose a delicious pasta dish made to order. Reservations recommended.

Taco Del Mar
350 E Main St • Pullman • (509) 334-7822
See review – Seattle

REPUBLIC

Ferry County Co-op
34 N Clark Street • Republic • (509) 775-3754

A natural foods co-op selling fresh produce, frozen vegetarian foods, packaged goods, and bulk foods. The fresh deli is mostly vegetarian. Open Mon-Fri 7:45am-6pm, Sat 10am-4pm. Closed Sun.

RICHLAND

DINING

Amici's Restaurant
94 Lee Blvd • Richland • (509) 942-1914

VegFriendly • Italian • Mon-Sat lunch & dinner • Closed Sun

Many dishes on the menu can be made vegetarian or vegan as you need. Try the Wild Mushroom Ravioli or specify your choice of pasta dish with vegetables. Excellent wine selections. For much of the year there is outside seating overlooking the Columbia River.

Emerald of Siam Thai Restaurant
1314 Jadwin Avenue • Richland • (509) 946-9328 • www.emeraldofsiam.com

VegFriendly • Thai • Mon-Fri lunch • Mon-Sat dinner • Closed Sun • Entrees $7-$9

There's a whole page of vegetarian options at this popular Thai restaurant, with traditional favorites such as Tofu Bathing Rama, red or green curry or noodle dishes. Be sure to specify your dietary requirements since some chicken or fish stock is used, but can be omitted on request.

FROM THE FARM

Market at the Parkway
Friday, 9am-1pm, June-September
The Parkway on Lee Blvd

Eastern Washington

ROSLYN

Roslyn Sunday Market
Sunday, 10am-1pm, June-September
Pennsylvania Ave at 1st St (Hwy 903)
www.RoslynMarkets.com

SPOKANE

DINING

9th Street Bistro
926 S Monroe St • Spokane • (509) 624-1349
www.huckleberrysnaturalmarket.com

VeryVegFriendly • American • Daily 7am-9pm • Full service or food bar • Entrees $5-$8

Inside Huckleberry's Natural Market is a full service Bistro, where you can enjoy delicious freshly made-to-order meals. Choose multigrain pancakes or tofu scramble for breakfast, a veggie burrito, soups or veggie burgers for lunch or build your own meal from the Meal Component bar, featuring many fresh vegetarian foods from which to choose.

Mizuna
214 N Howard St • Spokane • (509) 747-2004 • www.mizuna.com

VeryVegFriendly • Eclectic • Lunch Mon-Fri • Daily dinner • Full service
Entrees $15-$20

Sitting next to old brick walls, with candles on the table, you can enjoy a wide selection of vegetarian and vegan choices from their separate vegetarian menu. Many of their traditional main dishes are offered with meat substitutes such as tofu, tempeh, or Field Roast. Try Tofu fritters with hominy succotash or House made red curry with Small Planet Tofu. There is a selection of organic wines.

Niko's Greek Restaurant & Wine Bar
725 W Riverside Ave • Spokane • (509) 624 7444 • www.nikosspokane.com

VegFriendly • Greek • Daily dinner • Full service • Entrees $15-20

This upscale restaurant has a selection of vegetarian options such as spanakopita, feta fettuccine and Portobello with garlic mashed potatoes.

Peking Palace
11110 E Sprague Ave • Spokane • (509) 924-3933
www.pekingpalacespokane.com

VegFriendly • Chinese • Daily lunch & dinner • Entrées $5-10

Chinese without MSG. All the traditional dishes available with vegetables, such as Vegetable Chow Mein, Lo Mein, Chop Suey or Fried Rice, and some special vegetable and tofu dishes. Tofu can be substituted for meat in any dish.

Taco Del Mar
808 W Main Ave • Spokane • (509) 456-2237 • www.tacodelmar.com
12501 N Hwy 395 • Spokane • (509) 466-4814
509 N Sullivan Rd • Spokane • (509) 924-2252
8801 N Indian Trails Rd • Spokane • (509) 465-0760
3007 E 57th Ave • Spokane • (509) 443-1404
See review – Seattle

SHOPPING

Adventist Book Center
3715 S Grove Rd • Spokane • (800) 286-0161

Very popular with the vegetarian community. A large selection of vegetarian foods, including very wide choice of meat substitutes such as hot dogs, chicken, etc. Dried fruits, healthy snack foods, cereals, soy milks, soups, etc., are also available. Extensive selection of books on health, nutrition, and cookbooks. Open Mon-Thurs 9am-5:30pm, Sun 10am-3pm. Closed Fri & Sat.

Huckleberry's Natural Market
926 S Monroe St • Spokane • (509) 624-1349
www.huckleberrysnaturalmarket.com

A large store with a large range of high quality organic foods and a wide selection of organic produce. The Bistro has many freshly prepared soups, sandwiches, salads and hot off the line foods. The bakery has pastries, breads, muffins, pies, and cakes. Welcoming ambience, friendly and knowledgeable staff. Open daily 7am-10pm.

Lorien Herbs and Natural Foods
1102 S. Perry St • Spokane • (509) 456-0702

Twenty five years ago, Lorien became Spokane's first natural food store. It carries the largest selection of bulk herbs in the Inland Empire and quality supplements, remedies, books, and beauty products. All produce is certified organic. There is an experienced staff for personal help in selection. Open Tues-Fri 10am-6pm, Sat 10am-5pm. Closed Sun & Mon.

FROM THE FARM

Humble Earth Farmers' Market
Sunday, 10am-3pm, June-October
10505 Newport
www.spokanefarmersmarket.org

Liberty Lake Farmers' Market
Saturday, 9am-1pm, May-September
Liberty Square parking lot, 1421 N Meadowwood

South Perry Farmers' Market
Thursday, 3pm-7pm, June-September
1317 East 12th

Saturday, 8am-1pm, May-October
2nd Ave between Division and Browne

Spokane Farmers' Market
Wednesday, 8am-1pm, June-October
2nd Ave between Division and Browne

TONASKET

Tonasket Natural Foods Co-op
21 W 4th St • Tonasket • (509) 486-4188

A unique store in this rural area. The deli regularly prepares vegetarian soups, hot entrees, sandwiches, and salads. The produce cooler looks like a garden of organic vegetables. A large percentage is grown locally. They also carry organic foods, bulk items, health and beauty aids. Lunch in the garden gazebo. Open Mon-Sat 9am-6pm (7pm in summer), Sun 12-4pm.

WALLA WALLA

SHOPPING

Asia Oriental Store
1922 E Isaacs Ave • Walla Walla • (509) 527-0716

A small store selling all kinds of Asian food. Tofu, noodles, sauces, frozen vegetables, and prepared items such as potstickers and spring rolls are all available. Open Sun-Fri 11-6pm. Closed Sat.

Super 1 Foods
710 S 9th Ave (Hwy 125) • Walla Walla • (509) 525-8790

Inside this regular grocery store is a special natural-foods department, sponsored by Huckleberry's Natural Market. They sell packaged foods, frozen and refrigerated vegetarian and vegan foods and bulk items. The grocery store sells a wide range of fresh fruits and vegetables. Open 24hrs.

FROM THE FARM

Walla Walla Farmers' Market
Saturday and Sunday, 9am-1pm, May-October
City Hall Parking Lot, 4th & Main Street
www.gowallawallafarmersmarket.com

WENATCHEE

Taco Del Mar
142 Easy St • Wenatchee • (509) 665-9500
403 Valley Mall Parkway • Wenatchee • (509) 888-8226
See review – Seattle

Wenatchee Valley Farmers' Markets
Wednesday, 8am-1pm, June-October
Saturday, 8am-1pm, May-October
Sunday, 9am-1pm, July-October
Riverfront Park at the base of 5th Street

Thursday 4pm-7pm, June-October
Methow Park at Spokane & Methow Streets
www.wenatcheefarmersmarket.com

YAKIMA

DINING

El Porton
420 S 48th Ave • Yakima • (509) 965-5422

VeryVegFriendly • Mexican Family • Daily lunch & dinner

"Healthier Dishes" are showcased as a separate, totally vegetarian part of the extensive menu. Try Fajita Vegetarian, a huge sizzling pan with a bright variety of eight roasted vegetables with rice and beans and choice of corn or flour tortillas; it's vegan if you ask for no cheese and sour cream. The mystery spiced Cheese and Spinach Enchilada is excellent, as is the Chile Relleno, a rich mild poblano wrapped in the right balance of inner and outer flavors. Vegan Margarita!

Taco Del Mar
1300 N 40th Ave • Yakima • (509) 575-8997
See review – Seattle

SHOPPING

Rosauers Food & Drug Center
410 S 72nd Ave • Yakima • (509) 972-2327

Inside this regular grocery store is a special natural-foods department, sponsored by Huckleberry's Natural Market. They sell packaged foods, frozen and refrigerated vegetarian and vegan foods and bulk items. The grocery store sells a wide range of fresh fruits and vegetables. Open 5am-Midnight.

FROM THE FARM

Yakima Farmers' Market
Sunday, 9am-3pm, May-October
S 3rd Street at Yakima Avenue in front of Capitol Theatre

ZILLAH

El Porton
905 Vintage Valley Pkwy • Zillah • (509) 829-9100
See review – Yakima

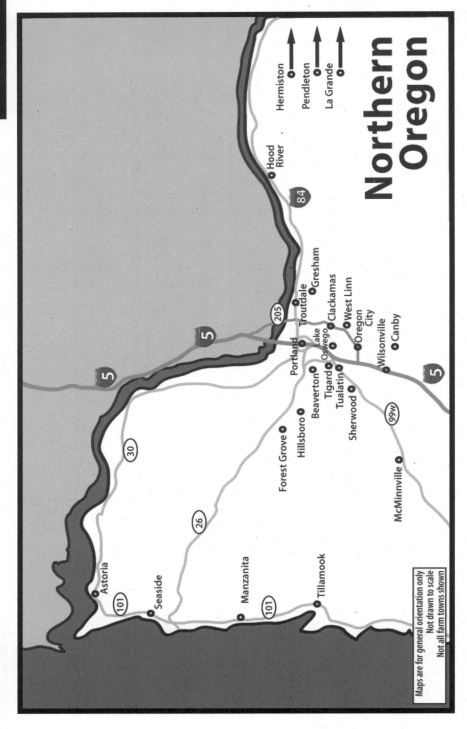

Northern Oregon

Hermiston

Pendleton

La Grande

Hood River

84

Gresham

Troutdale

205

Clackamas

West Linn

Lake
Oswego

Oregon
City

5

Portland

Wilsonville

Canby

Beaverton

Tigard

Tualatin

Sherwood

5

Hillsboro

99w

Forest Grove

30

McMinnville

26

Manzanita

Astoria

101

Seaside

Tillamook

101

Maps are for general orientation only
Not drawn to scale
Not all farm towns shown

Northern Oregon

ASTORIA

DINING

The Columbian Café
1114 Marine Dr • Astoria • (503) 325-2233

VeryVegFriendly • Natural foods • Full service • Breakfast & lunch daily
Dinner Wed-Sat

This small bohemian restaurant is vegetarian apart from the few fish entrees offered for dinner. There are plenty of delicious meals to choose from including rice,
vegetable and tofu dishes, bean burritos, homemade pasta, and other international
options. Salsas are made from all types of fruits and vegetables. Delicious crepes
with a variety of fillings, vegan chili, and French onion soup are their specialties.

SHOPPING

Astoria Cooperative
1389 Duane St • Astoria • (503) 325-0027 • www.astoriacoop.org

Astoria Cooperative is a small natural foods cooperative grocery. Provides a wide
selection of sustainably produced, fairly traded and organically grown products,
with emphasis on the locally grown. The store is open to the public and provides
discounts to co-op members. Open Mon-Sat 9am-7pm, Sun 11am-5pm.

Astoria Health Foods
1255 Commercial St • Astoria • (503) 325-6688

This small store located in the heart of downtown Astoria carries a large variety of
supplements, homeopathic remedies, bulk herbs and foods, teas, snacks, books and
beauty aids. Plentiful selection of packaged, frozen, and refrigerated foods for the
vegan/vegetarian palate. Friendly, approachable staff willing to research information
and accommodate special orders. Open Mon-Fri 9am-5:30pm, Sat 9am-6pm.

FROM THE FARM

Astoria Sunday Market
Sundays, 10am-3pm, May-October
Downtown Astoria at 12th St & Marine Dr.

BEAVERTON

DINING

India Direct

16205 NW Bethany Ct • Beaverton • (503) 690-0499
www.shopindiadirect.com

Vegetarian • Indian • Lunch and dinner • Full service & take out • Entrees $5-10
Closed Mon

India Direct is an Indian grocery store with a small café in the back. The menu is limited but 100% vegetarian. The food is incredibly good but a little spicy. India Direct caters to the local Indian community so the food is authentic. Seating is at the counters, barstool style. The café seats only about 10 people. If you have to wait, you can do some grocery shopping in the store where you can find every kind of spice imaginable.

Swagat Indian Cuisine

4325 SW 109th Ave • Beaverton • (503) 626-3000 • www.indogram.com/swagat

VegFriendly • Indian • Daily lunch (buffet) & dinner • Full service & take out
Entrees $5-10

The full range of traditional north and south Indian dishes are offered at this traditional Indian restaurant, but their specialties are from Madras and southeast India. The classic lentil flour dosas are crepe-style pancakes, over a foot wide, which are stuffed with a vegetable curry. The all-you-can-eat buffet is a great choice for lunch.

Sweet Tomatoes

1225 NW Waterhouse Ave • Beaverton • (503) 439-0850
www.sweettomatoes.com

VeryVegFriendly • Soups, Salad & Pasta • Daily lunch & dinner

Sweet Tomatoes is a family-friendly, self-serve, salad-buffet restaurant offering much more than just salad. All items have very clearly marked ingredients and there are many vegetarian and vegan options. You can go back for seconds so bring an appetite. The atmosphere is light and cheerful. Take out is available. The staff is helpful and parking is very convenient.

Taco Del Mar

9454 SW Allen Blvd • Beaverton • (503) 293-0030 • www.tacodelmar.com

VeryVegFriendly • Lunch & dinner • Entrees under $5

Vegan fast food? Yes, it's true! Try Taco Del Mar for a colorful, fun restaurant known for fresh and quality ingredients as well as healthy fast food alternatives. There are many vegetarian options and a vegan burrito right on the menu. Don't forget to try the smoothies and the chips and salsa—they are excellent. The friendly staff will quickly prepare your food right in front of you. Perfect for kids.

Thai Orchid Restaurant
18070 NW Evergreen Pkwy • Beaverton • (503) 439-6683
16165 SW Regatta Ln • Beaverton • (503) 617-4602
www.thaiorchidrestaurant.com

VegFriendly • Thai • Daily lunch & dinner • Full service • Entrees $5-10

Traditional Thai food that is fresh, flavorful and healthy with no MSG or hydrogenated oil added. Choose from more than 40 vegetarian options including choices such as Pad Nam Prik Phao (with chili jam, eggplant, bell peppers, onions, and sweet basil leaves), Gaeng Pa Nang (with Pa Nang curry, green beans, and kaffir leaves) and the traditional Pad Thai. Level of spiciness can be prepared to your liking.

SHOPPING

New Seasons Market
3495 Cedar Hills Blvd • Beaverton • (503) 641-4181
See description – Portland

Trader Joe's
11753 SW Beaverton Hillsdale Hwy • Beaverton • (503) 626-3794
www.traderjoes.com
See description – Portland

Uwajimaya
10500 SW Beaverton Hillsdale Hwy • Beaverton • (503) 643-4512
www.uwajimaya.com

An excellent source for Asian specialties, spices, vegetarian and vegan items. Large produce section includes organic produce. Gifts, household items, cookware. Inside the store is Hakatamon Restaurant where Chef Kato makes fresh udon noodles by hand daily for delicious soups. Restaurant, bakery items and deli items, too. Open 9am-10pm Monday-Saturday, Sunday 9am-9pm.

Wild Oats Natural Marketplace
4000 SW 117th Ave • Beaverton • (503) 646-3824 • www.wildoats.com
See description – Portland

FROM THE FARM

Beaverton Farmers' Markets
Wednesdays, 3pm-6pm, Mid June-August
Saturdays, 8am-1:30pm, Mid May-October
Hall Blvd, between 3rd & 5th Streets
www.beavertonfarmersmarket.com

BORING

Boring Farmers' Market
Sunday, 9am-2pm, June-Early September
Boring Station Trailhead Park, Hwy 212 and Wally Rd

CANBY

Canby Saturday Farmers' Market
Saturdays, 9am-1pm, Mid May-Mid October
1st Ave at Holly Street

Natural Harvest Farm
PO Box 1106 • Canby • (503) 916-9198
www.osalt.org/csa_at_natural_harvest_farm.html

Natural Harvest grows vegetables, fruits, herbs & flowers for pickup at the farm,
Farmers' Market, or at Peoples Co-op weekly or bi-weekly from March through
November.

CEDAR MILL

Cedar Mill Sunset Farmers' Market
Saturdays, 8am-1pm
NW Cornell, 1 block West of Murray across from Sunset High School
www.cmfmarket.org

CLACKAMAS

DINING

Sweet Tomatoes
13011 SE 84th Ave • Clackamas • (503) 794-2921 • www.sweettomatoes.com
See review – Beaverton

Taco Del Mar
9968 SE 82nd Ave • Clackamas • (503) 771-2775 • www.tacodelmar.com
See review – Beaverton

SHOPPING

Adventist Book Center
13455 SE 97th Ave • Clackamas • (503) 653-0978

Very popular with the vegetarian community. A large selection of vegetarian foods,
including a very wide choice of vegetarian meat replacement foods such as analogs
for chili, hot dogs, burgers, etc. Organic foods, dried fruits, healthy snack foods,

cereals, soy milks, soups, etc. Books on health and nutrition and cookbooks. Open Mon-Thurs 9am-6pm, Fri 9am-1pm, Sun 11am-4pm.

DUNDEE

Dundee Farmers' Market
Sunday, 10am-2pm, Mid May-Early October
Hwy 99 and 7th Street

ENTERPRISE

Enterprise Farmers' Market
Thursday, 4pm-7pm, June-Mid September
County Courthouse Lawn
www.neofm.org/blog/Joseph

ESTACADA

Estacada Farmers' Market
Saturdays, 9am-2pm, Mid May-October
3rd & Broadway St
www.estacadafarmersmarket.4t.com

FAIRVIEW

Fairview Farmers' & Artist Market
Thursday, 4pm-8pm, April-Mid October
Fairview City Hall, 1300 Village St.

FOREST GROVE

FROM THE FARM

Forest Grove & Adelante Mujeres Farmers' Market
Wednesday, 4pm-8pm, Mid May-Mid October
21st Avenue, between College & Main

Love Farm Organics
46125 NW Hillside Road • Forest Grove • (503) 515-9939
www.lovefarmorganics.com

A summer share CSA of 25 weeks begins the day after Mother's Day through Halloween and provides vegetables, salad greens mix, herbs, flowers, berries, and other fruits. Bulk orders for berries. Pick up Monday evenings at the farm. Delivery Thursday evenings in the Garden Home/Hillsdale area.

Morning Star Farm

5755 Thatcher Road • Forest Grove • (503) 357-7886 • www.morningstarfarm.org

Vegetables, herbs and fruit are certified organically grown by Oregon Tilth. CSA pick-up is at the farm June through October.

Sun Gold Farm

6995 NW Evers Rd • Forest Grove • (503) 357-3851 • www.sungoldfarm.com

This family farm grows fresh market crops of vegetables, fruits, herbs and flowers which they sell directly to the consumer at various farmers' markets and through their "Harvest Box" program, also known as a CSA. All crops are grown without pesticides. They control weeds by mulching, rototilling, hoeing, and "going down on our knees and pulling!" Delivery throughout the Beaverton/Portland area.

GRESHAM

DINING

Taco Del Mar

2469 SE Burnside Rd • Gresham • (503) 674-9867 • www.tacodelmar.com
See review – Beaverton

Thai Orchid Restaurant

120 N Main Ave • Gresham • (503) 491-0737 • www.thaiorchidrestaurant.com
See review – Beaverton

SHOPPING

Wild Oats Natural Marketplace

2077 NE Burnside Rd • Gresham • (503) 674-2827 • www.wildoats.com
See description – Portland

FROM THE FARM

Gresham Farmers' Market

Saturdays, 8:30am-2pm, May-October
Miller Street between 2nd & 3rd
www.greshamfarmersmarket.com

HILLSBORO

DINING

Taco Del Mar
48th & Cornell • Hillsboro • (503) 648-3424 • www.tacodelmar.com
110 SE Washington • Hillsboro • (503) 640-8205
22095 NW Inbrie Dr • Hillsboro • (503) 648-3337
See review – Beaverton

Thai Orchid Restaurant
4550 NE Cornell Rd • Hillsboro • (503) 681-2611
www.thaiorchidrestaurant.com
See review – Beaverton

Swagath
1340 NE Orenco Station Parkway • Hillsboro • (503) 844-3838 • www.swagat.com

VegFriendly • Indian • Daily lunch & dinner • Entrees $5-10

Sister restaurant to the Swagat restaurants in Portland and Beaverton, Swagath is a traditional-style Indian restaurant offering both northern and southern styles of cuisine. The decorations and music create an authentic atmosphere and the service is helpful. The staff is eager to explain ingredients and make suggestions for vegan options. Try the Aloo Gobi with whole wheat Roti. Lunch buffet available.

SHOPPING

New Seasons Market
1453 NE 61st Ave • Hillsboro • (503) 648-6968
See description – Portland

Trader Joe's
2285 NW 185th Ave • Hillsboro • (503) 645-8321
See description – Portland

FROM THE FARM

Hillsboro Farmers' Markets
Tuesdays, 5pm-8:30pm, Mid June-August
Courthouse Square Main St., 1st to 3rd Ave

Saturdays, 8am-1:30pm, May-December
Courthouse Square, 2nd & East Main

Sundays, 10am-2pm Mid May-October
Orenco Station, NW Cornell Rd and Orenco Station Pkwy
www.hillsboromarkets.org

La Finquita del Buho

7960 NW Dick Rd • Hillsboro • (503) 647-2595

A small family-run CSA using organic practices. CSA subscribers get weekly vegetable and fruit baskets from April through October. Pickup is at the farm and families are welcome for a tour of the farm and a chance to help on a working farm. The 28-30 week season runs from April-October.

HERMISTON

Hermiston Farmers' Market

Saturdays, 9am-1pm, Mid May-Early October
Hermiston Conference Center Parking Lot, Hwy 395
www.neorfm.org/blog/Hermiston

HOOD RIVER

DINING

China Gorge Restaurant

2680 Old Columbia River Dr • Hood River • (541) 386-5331
www.chinagorge.com

VegFriendly • Szechwan & Hunan • Lunch & dinner • Closed Mon

Enthusiastically, "Oh yes, we have lots of vegetarian foods. We serve tempeh, our eggrolls are vegetarian, lots of vegetarian Chow Meins and many other things like Crispy Eggplant." Locals love it. Just east of downtown, across the Hood River with a view of the Columbia River. Vegan options.

Mother's Market Place

106 Highway 35 • Hood River • (541) 387-2202

Vegan • Home cooking • Tiny counter & take out • Closed Fri at 3pm & Sat

Inside this small vegan store is a great place to pick up quick, hot, freshly prepared and self-serve vegan eats like fresh steamed tamales, creamy (nut cream) asparagus soup, or vegan pizza. Sandwiches are available in the summer. There is a fresh juice bar, and you could eat at the tiny counter which overlooks the Columbia River.

Sixth St Bistro and Loft

509 Cascade • Hood River • (541) 386-5737

VegFriendly • Northwest eclectic • Daily lunch & dinner • Entrees $10-20

Menu varies with the season. Some vegetarian choices always available and they are all extraordinary, like the local wild mushrooms from the nearby forests. Classic meat-based dishes can be made with tofu. Many appetizers are actually vegan. You can "veg out" with their artichoke dip, rustic bread, and the huge and succulent seasonal greens salad. The menu celebrates the foragers, farmers, and orchards who supply them (all organic). Cozy restaurant under, happy bistro above with vegan microbrews!

Taco Del Mar
112 Oak St • Hood River • (541) 308-0033 • www.tacodelmar.com
See review – Beaverton

FROM THE FARM

Gorge Grown Farmers' Market
Thursday, 4pm-7pm, Mid June-Early October
Hood River Middle School, 1602 May St
www.gorgegrown.com/farmersmarket.cfm

Saturday Market, 9am-3pm, May-September
5th and Columbia, across from Full Sail
www.community.gorge.net/saturdaymarket

JOSEPH

Joseph Farmers' Market
Saturdays, 9am-1pm, June-Mid October
Corner of Main and Joseph St
www.neofm.org/blog/Joseph

LAKE OSWEGO

DINING

Taco Del Mar
15170 SW Bangy Rd • Lake Oswego • (503) 968 6968 • www.tacodelmar.com
See review – Beaverton

SHOPPING

New Seasons Market
3 SW Monroe Parkway • Lake Oswego • (503) 496-1155
See description – Portland

Trader Joe's
15391 SW Bangy Rd • Lake Oswego • (503) 639-3238 • www.traderjoes.com
See description – Portland

Wild Oats Natural Marketplace
17711 Jean Way • Lake Oswego • (503) 635-8950 • www.wildoats.com
See description – Portland

FROM THE FARM

Lake Oswego Farmers' Market
Saturdays, 8:30am-1:30pm, Mid May-Mid October
Millennium Park, 1st & Evergreen
www.ci.oswego.or.us

LA GRANDE

La Grande Farmers' Market
Tuesdays, 4pm-6pm, July-Early September
4th & Adams

Saturdays, 9am-12 noon, Mid May-End of October
Max Square, 4th & Adams
www.neofm.org/blog/LaGrande

MANZANITA

Mother Nature's Natural Foods
298 Laneda Ave • Manzanita • (503) 368-5316
www.neahkahnie.net/mothernatures/index.html

Located three blocks from the beach, this progressive little natural food store has a creative floor plan and unique product selection that will delight you! Packed with stunning organic produce, a mighty bulk selection, wine/beer, books, and specialty grocery. There's an organic juice bar and deli to go, spelt fruit muffins made daily, fair trade chocolate and coffee, and a welcoming down-to-earth staff. Open daily 10am-7pm.

Manzanita Farmers' Market
Fridays, 5pm-8pm, End of June-Mid September
Hwy 101 & Alder St

McMINNVILLE

DINING

Wild Wood Café
319 N Baker St • McMinnville • (503) 435-1454

VegFriendly • Café • Daily breakfast & lunch • Full service

Family-owned restaurant specializing in breakfast. Try the Wild Wood toast with granola, a potato plate, or an omelet with avocado, olives, salsa, and cheddar cheese. A wide range of veggie burgers, veggie melts, and salads are available for lunch. They make their own breads, granola, soups, and salsa.

FROM THE FARM

McMinnville Farmers' Market

Thursdays, 1:30pm-6:30pm, June-Mid October
Cowls Street, between 2nd & 3rd
www.downtownmcminnville.com

Oakhill Organics

PO Box 1698 • McMinnville • (503) 474-7661 • www.oakhillorganics.org

This 17-acre vegetable farm is nestled between two branches of the Willamette
River on Grand Island south of McMinnville and north of Salem. They sell through
their Community Supported Agriculture (CSA) program, at the McMinnville
Farmers' Market, and through custom harvests. These are fulltime vegetable growers in their third season growing a broad and diverse mix of vegetables. This is an
organic farm, certified by Oregon Tilth.

MILWAUKIE

Milwaukie Sunday Farmers' Market

Sundays, 9:30am-2pm, Mid May-October
SE Main between Harrison & Jackson Streets across from City Hall
www.milwaukiefarmersmarket.com

NORTH PLAINS

Dos Sequoias Farm

10440 NW Jackson Quarry Rd • Hillsboro • (503) 261-0640
www.abundantharvest.biz

This is a partnership between two families, one family who owns the farm and the
other family who are the produce growers. They produce an assortment of vegetables, herbs, some fruit, and flowers which are grown from June to November.
The produce is harvested at its peak of flavor and nutrition in the morning for
CSA member pickup that afternoon. The farm is on five beautiful acres of Oregon's
prime farmland.

Pumpkin Ridge Gardens

31067 Pumpkin Ridge Dr • North Plains • (503) 647-5023
www.PumpkinRidgeGardens.com

One of the few area farms that grows and delivers fresh vegetables year-round for
a limited number of subscribers. Vegetables and herbs are harvested on the day
they are delivered. This CSA becomes the core of a seasonal diet for all 12 months.
Each share is sufficient for two to four people for a nutritionally balanced mixture
that includes some unusual varieties as well as perennial favorites. All vegetables are
grown without using artificial fertilizers or pesticides.

OREGON CITY

DINING

Taco Del Mar
19526 Molalla Ave • Oregon City • (503) 518 8226 • www.tacodelmar.ocm
See review – Beaverton

FROM THE FARM

Birds & Bees Community Farm
20495 S Geiger Road • Oregon City • (503) 655-7447

Year-round CSA offering vegetables, fruit, honey, and herbs using sustainable farming methods. Pickup is at the farm which is part of Mahonia Land Trust Conservancy.

Oregon City Farmers' Market
Saturdays, 9am-2pm, May-October
Clackamas County Public Service Parking Lot, 2051 Kaen Rd. at Beavercreek Rd
www.orcityfarmersmarket.com

PENDLETON

Pendleton Farmers' Market
Fridays, 4pm-8pm (or until dusk), Mid May-Mid October
S Main St. between Emigrant & Frazer St
www.pendletonfarmersmarket.net

PORTLAND

DINING

Abou Karim
221 SW Pine St • Portland • (503) 223-5058

VeryVegFriendly • Middle Eastern • Daily Lunch & dinner Fri-Sat • Full service
Entrees $5-10

Their vegetarian specialties are at the top of the menu but much of this authentic Lebanese cuisine is actually vegan. Try a whole plate full of appetizers called the Mezza, spoon up some Lentil Soup and make a main dish of Falafel, those crispy deep fried (vegetable oil) patties of herbed and spiced garbanzo and fava flour. Vegans can skip the yogurt sauce. Friendly, cozy.

Backspace Cafe

115 NW 5th Ave • Portland • (503) 248-2900 • www.backspace.bz

Vegetarian • Café • Daily lunch & dinner • Counter service & take out
Entrees $5-10

Backspace Cafe is a spacious 4,000 square foot Internet cafe, art gallery, and gaming spot in downtown Portland. Their mostly vegan menu features sandwiches, salads, soups, and snacks. All items can be made vegan upon request, and they offer items such as Tofutti cream cheese and Follow Your Heart cheese and Vegenaise. Menu options include quesadillas, a number of Field Roast sandwiches, and pizza and calzones prepared by Hot Lips Pizza. Note that to-go orders are subject to a twenty-five-cent fee to offset costs of environmentally friendly packaging.

Bayleaf Vegetarian Restaurant

4768 SE Division Street • Portland • (503) 232-7058 • www.bayleafvegetarian.com

Vegetarian • Pan-Asian • Daily lunch & dinner • Full service

The Bay Leaf is a relatively new and quite authentic Chinese vegetarian restaurant. The atmosphere is elegant and the service excellent. The menu offers an extensive number of choices featuring some of the best vegetarian dishes in region. Both faux meat and whole food vegetable dishes are featured at what has quickly become one of Portland's most popular vegetarian restaurants. Take out is available and parking is convenient. This is a great restaurant for special occasions as well as every day dining.

Blue Moose Café

4936 NE Fremont St • Portland • (503) 548-4475 • www.portlandbluemoose.com

Vegetarian • American • Mon-Fri for lunch & dinner and Sat-Sun for three meals
Full service & take out • Credit cards accepted • Entrees $5-10

Like walking into a vegetarian version of Mom's kitchen, the Blue Moose Café serves an array of familiar dishes as well as creative yet very approachable plates. Upon being seated at the warm, cozy tables the friendly server offers a sample of the day's soup. Breakfast is served all day, including vegan pancakes, tofu scrambles, and breakfast burritos. Wholesome and nutritious foods like special salads and vegetable medleys dominate the well-rounded menu. Most of their delectable deserts are surprisingly vegan, especially the extra creamy homemade soy ice cream that leaves you wondering if they accidentally served the cow's-milk version.

Bombay Cricket Club

1925 SE Hawthorne Blvd • Portland • (503) 231-0740

VegFriendly • Indian • Daily for dinner • Full service & take out • Entrees $5-10

Often praised by critics as the best Indian restaurant in Portland, it has earned its reputation by delivering exceptional food and outstanding service in a warm atmosphere. On top of several delicious varieties of naan bread, they also offer a selection of Mediterranean appetizers. The dishes are prepared with delicate attention and will leave you satisfied. Romantic. Make a reservation before the rest of Portland does.

Bye and Bye

1011 NE Alberta St • Portland • (503) 281-0537
www.myspace.com/byeandbyeportland

Vegan • Bar/American • Daily dinner • Counter service & take out • Entrees $6-8

Bye and Bye is a hip bar/restaurant serving all-vegan Southern-style food. Although the main focus is the bar, the food itself is worth the visit. BBQ "Chicken," an Eastern bowl, and a popular meatball sub are a few of the gems that grace the small but intelligent menu. All eight entrees come with a choice of sides which include black-eyed peas and greens. The dining area is dimly lit, lending to the modern, stylized atmosphere, and is divided into small intimate spaces. A beautiful back patio and the spacious, nonsmoking quarters inside, combined with the compassionately delicious menu, are sure to create an enjoyable night out.

Caffe Mingo

807 NW 21st Ave • Portland • (503) 226-4646

VegFriendly • Italian • Dinner daily • Entrees $10-20

One of the city's most cherished Italian restaurants. It features outstanding, hearty, meatless entrees and antipasti like penne alla zucca, asparagus or mushroom ravioli with walnut sauce, baked semolina gnocchi, and a spinach and roasted beet salad. All wonderful things you can anticipate as you dip chunks of wonderfully chewy bread into a big bowl of juicy olives. Racks of wine bottles climb the walls, for what is Italian food without wine? To finish, try their classic panna cotta "cooked cream" dessert with poached fruit or a simple dish of gelato.

Chaos Café and Parlor

2620 SE Powell Blvd • Portland • (503) 546-8112

Vegetarian • American • Mon – Sat breakfast, lunch & dinner • Closed Sun
Entrees $5-$10

The Chaos Café and Parlor offers vegetarian, American-style cuisine with many vegan options emphasizing local and fresh ingredients. Beverages include signature juices and smoothies. The atmosphere is cheerful and the restaurant is well decorated. The menu was fun to read and baby boomers will recognize many of their favorite icons of the 60's. There's live music most evenings. The service is friendly and there is a free parking lot half a block east of the restaurant.

Cup & Saucer Café
3000 NE Killingsworth • Portland • (503) 287-4427
3566 SE Hawthorne Blvd • Portland • (503) 236-6001

VegFriendly • American • Open daily for three meals • Full service & take out
Entrees $5-10

Traditional lunches and hearty breakfasts are served all day. Vegans can enjoy a few different foods, including cornmeal pancakes, cranberry apple coffee cake, carrot cake and home fried potatoes. Tofu may be substituted for eggs in their scrambles. The atmosphere is laid-back and artsy in this diner/café.

Divine Café
SW 9th Ave, between Washington & Alder • Portland • (503) 314-9606

Vegetarian • A cart • Mon-Fri lunch • Closed Sat-Sun • Take out

This cart serves vegetarian and vegan meals, such as smoked-tofu sandwiches and soba salad in peanut sauce. Vegan desserts are also available.

Dot's Café
2521 SE Clinton St • Portland • (503) 235-0203

VegFriendly • American/Mexican • Daily lunch, dinner & late night • Full service & take out • Entrees $5-10

A unique, reinvigorated diner with a hip lounge motif serving diner fare with a unique twist. The funky, dimly lit, eclectic atmosphere is as much of an attraction as the food. A handful of items are labeled as vegan. Vegetarian options include a tasty hummus sandwich containing sautéed spinach and mushrooms, a vegan burrito platter, and Gardenburgers. They also offer vegan cake by the slice. Full cocktail bar with pool table. No minors after 10pm. Food is served until 2am. Smoking/non-smoking sections.

Garden Café at Portland Adventist Medical Center
10123 SE Market St • Portland • (503) 251-6125 • Closed Sat

Vegetarian • Cafeteria • Daily lunch & early dinner • Entrees under $5

Vegetarian meals have been served here for more than 100 years. Enjoy a wide variety of foods in a comfortable dining area with indoor and outdoor seating. Choose from vegetarian entrées such as chili macaroni, Singapore curry or cashew loaf. There's an extensive salad bar, a fresh fruit bar and a fast-food grill with vegetarian sandwiches and Boca burgers. The wide selection of beverages is all caffeine free.

Horn of Africa
5237 NE Martin Luther King Jr. Blvd • Portland • (503) 331-9844
www.hornofafrica.net

VegFriendly • East African • Lunch buffet and dinner • Closed Sun • Full service
Entrees $5-10

Authentic dishes from the Ethiopian region, using ingredients of exceptional quality, many of which are organic. Several vegan options are available. Try their veggie combo: fresh collard greens, mixed vegetables, creamy navy beans and organic red lentils, served with a salad, saffron rice and biddeena (homemade organic Horn-of-Africa-style spongy bread). The environment is casual and the service is friendly. You can also find a Horn of Africa food cart at the Portland Saturday (& Sunday) Market.

India Chaat House

804 SW 12th Ave • Portland • (503) 241-7944

Vegetarian • Cart/Indian • Daily lunch & dinner • Credit cards not accepted
Entrees $5-10

This all-vegetarian Indian food cart features a large selection of dishes, including a $5 lunch special which is entirely vegan. The prices are very reasonable and the portions are extremely generous. There is a small, covered seating area with two tables but it's mostly take-away. Some claim this is the best Indian food in town. Come hungry or share the lunch special with a friend!

India Grill

2924 E Burnside St • Portland • (503) 236-1790

VegFriendly • Indian • Daily lunch & dinner • Full service & take out
Entrees $8-10

India Grill has an eclectic range of delicious dishes, with part of its menu being vegetarian specials. Favorites include Navratan curry (mixed vegetables), okra with onions, and vegetable biryani.

Iron Horse Restaurant

6034 SE Milwaukee Ave • Portland • (503) 232-1826
www.portlandironhorse.com

VegFriendly • Mexican • Lunch & dinner • Closed Mon • Full service & take out
Entrees $5-10

This large restaurant is both a vegetarian- and Mexican-food-lover's delight. Standard Southwestern and Mexican dishes are prepared to a scrumptious perfection, making them anything but standard. As soon as you get to your table you are greeted with a smile, chips and some of the best salsa in Portland. The vegetable chimichanga is a treat stuffed with zucchini, carrots, mushrooms, and guacamole. A vegan menu is available upon request.

It's a Beautiful Pizza

3342 SE Belmont Street • Portland • (503) 233-5444

VegFriendly • Pizza • Daily lunch & dinner • Full service & take out
Entrees $10-20

This popular pizza restaurant offers a wide variety of toppings including artichoke hearts, pine nuts, broccoli, spinach, and sundried tomatoes. You may substitute tofu for chicken, and soy cheese may be substituted for cheese on any pizza for the price of an additional topping. Pizzas are named after classic rock legends, including Joni Mitchell and Janis Joplin, and four vegetarian specialty pizzas are offered. The atmosphere has a 1960's feel with decorations of unique murals and large wall hangings. Live music can be heard on certain days of the week.

Jam On Hawthorne

2239 SE Hawthorne • Portland • (503) 234-4790

VeryVegFriendly • American style café • Breakfast/brunch • Full service & take out
Entrees $5-10

This classic brunch joint honors the eclectic countercultural spirit of Hawthorne Boulevard, serving organic coffee, homemade jam, a vegan tofu scramble, and tasty specialties such as lemon ricotta pancakes and a brie and mustard scramble, all served to the tunes of the Grateful Dead and Phish.

Kalga Kafé

4147 SE Division St • Portland • (503) 236-4770

Vegetarian • International • Daily dinner • Full service & take out • Entrees $5-10

A recent blessing to Portland's vegetarian scene with creative yet tasteful food served until midnight. Many of their dishes are naturally vegan and almost all can be made so. The cuisine ranges from Japanese to Mexican to Indian but don't rule out the pizza with a vegan cheese option. An eclectic and intimate setting where late night diners will enjoy DJ music under dim lights, and sip vegan chai served in a golden chalice.

Khun Pic's Bahn Thai

3429 SE Belmont St • Portland • (503) 235-1610

VeryVegFriendly • Thai • Dinner Tues-Sat • Closed Sun-Mon • Full service
Entrees $10-20 • No credit cards accepted

This is gourmet Thai with a short but powerful menu, virtually all of which is or can be vegetarian. The food is reported to be "fantastic" with the specialty here being that all the orders are prepared solely by Chef Khun Pic. Guests are urged to ask about the preparation time so that they can enjoy the leisure of conversation as their meal is custom cooked.

Laughing Planet Café

3320 SE Belmont Ave • Portland • (503) 235-6472

VeryVegFriendly • Juice Bar/Mexican • Daily for lunch & dinner
Counter service & take out • Entrees around $5

This juice bar/café offers many vegetarian and vegan options including fresh soups, veggie burgers, and quesadillas. Their build-your-own burritos include tofu, spinach, broccoli, brown rice, and other sustainable local farm products. All sauces are vegan and homemade. They offer vegan soy cheese and sour cream. Vegan desserts are available, including cookies and brownies. The atmosphere is fun and colorful, and the café claims a healthy community conscience that supports non-corporate local events and organizations.

Nicholas Restaurant

318 SE Grand Ave • Portland • (503) 235-5123 • www.nicholasrestaurant.com

VegFriendly • Lebanese/Middle East • Lunch & dinner • Full service and take out
Entrees $5-10

With a vast array of vegetarian options, this is a Portland mainstay for good reason. Set in a quaint old-world café, the food is as authentic as the rustic Lebanese décor. Veggie kabobs, falafel and mannakish, a pizza with oregano, thyme, sumac, olive oil, and sesame seeds, are all made deliciously. If you want to try it all, try the mezza platter. Specify either vegetarian or vegan and you will be rewarded with a generous assortment of their mouthwatering dishes. Their freshly baked pita bread is wonderful. High chairs are available.

Nutshell

3808 N Williams Ave • Portland • (503) 292-2627 • www.nutshellpdx.com

Vegan • International • Daily dinner • Full service & take out • Entrees $10-$16

Nutshell is an all-vegan restaurant featuring eclectic, creative, international dishes that focus on local, seasonal produce and do not contain soy or meat analogs. Entrees include Jamaican barbeque, Israeli couscous, and Warm Yukon Gold potato pancakes. They offer a complete bread, olive oil, and salt bar and you can even order shots of soup. Many of the items on Nutshell's menu are or can be made gluten-free. The atmosphere is hip, spacious, and modern with tall ceilings, large wooden booths and a front roll up garage-style window. Reservations are not accepted, so be prepared to wait for a table on busy evenings.

Oasis Café

3701 SE Hawthorne Blvd • Portland • (503) 231-0901

VegFriendly • Café • Daily lunch & dinner • Entrees $5-10

Oasis' specialty is pizza, with every possible combination of toppings. Try the veggie combo or the Hawthorne special, or design your own with your choice of toppings. An array of sandwiches, soups, salads, focaccia, and desserts is also available.

Old Wives' Tales

1300 E Burnside St • Portland • (503) 238-0470

VeryVegFriendly • Inventive • Daily for three meals • Full service & take out
Entrees $5-10

Large, family-style restaurant, with breakfast options served all day, plus extensive lunch and dinner choices. The menu is very helpful in explaining vegetarian or vegan dishes. Choices include Tofu Rancheros, Spicy Adobo Roasted Vegetables, Spanokopita, and delicious daily soups. Notable salad bar with unique dressings. Vegan dessert options. The service is friendly, with the feeling that the meals are home cooked. Very child friendly.

Paradox Palace Café

3439 SE Belmont St • Portland • (503) 232-7508

VeryVegFriendly • American • Daily three meals • Full service & take out
Entrees $5-10

This popular diner style café boasts an extensive variety of eclectic vegetarian/vegan dishes. Sharing the same owners as Vita Café across town, they specialize in meat-, dairy- and egg-free versions of classic dishes. Try their Tofurky Sandwich, Tempeh Broccoli Surprise, and Vegan Sloppy Joes. Breakfast items are available throughout the day and all breads and desserts are vegan.

Pepino's Fresh Mexican Grill

3832 SE Hawthorne Blvd • Portland • (503) 236-5000
914 NW 23rd Ave • Portland • (503) 226-9600

VeryVegFriendly • Mexican • Daily lunch & dinner • Entrees $5-10

Pepino's is not your usual burrito-and-taco restaurant. The menu offerings are especially creative. Try the Sweet Tequila Tofu Burrito and the Tofu Tortilla Soup. Also look for specials such as the Thai Veggie Burrito. Vegetarians will appreciate the no lard, no MSG, all-natural policy. Contemporary Mexican music rounds out the dining experience at this cheerful and quite popular restaurant. Parking is convenient behind the restaurant.

Plainfields' Mayur

852 SW 21st St • Portland • (503) 223-2995 • www.plainfields.com

VeryVegFriendly • Indian • Open daily for dinner • Full service & take out
Entrees $10-20

Formal, upscale, and elegant for a special dinner with exceptional food. Set in an opulent Victorian mansion where black-tie career waiters serve tables set with fine crystal, china, and full silver service. There is a glassed-in Tandoori show kitchen. The menu includes a delectable variety of traditional and original Indian cuisine, with about half the menu devoted to vegetarian or vegan dishes. Noted by many critics as one of the best Indian restaurants in the country. Reservations recommended.

Proper Eats Market and Café

8638 N Lombard St • Portland • (503) 445-2007 • www.propereats.org

Vegetarian • Café/International • Mon-Sat breakfast • Daily lunch & dinner
Counter service & take out • Entrees $5-10

Proper Eats Café and Market, located in the St. Johns section of North Portland, aims to bring locally grown, sustainable products to the community. The very vegan-friendly café features soups, salads, sandwiches, wraps, burritos, and entrees that draw upon a number of cultural influences. Menu items include a Tempeh Reuben sandwich, Raw Fajitas, and Sesame Peanut Noodles. The small market offers fresh, local produce, bulk items and a variety of other products. Local artists and musicians are featured regularly at the café.

Queen of Sheba

2413 NE Martin Luther King Jr Blvd • Portland • (503) 287-6302

VegFriendly • Ethiopian • Lunch Thurs-Sat • Daily dinner • Full service & take out
Entrees $5-10

Tasty Ethiopian delights including an excellent array of vegetarian dishes. If you feel there are just too many options, try their vegetarian sampler which includes 10 vegetarian dishes and a salad. You will be amazed that so many wonderful flavors can reside on one large piece of bread or injara. Authentic North African style with a broad assortment of unique dishes.

Sivalai

4806 Stark Street • Portland • (503) 230-2875

VeryVegFriendly • Thai • Daily lunch & dinner

Sivalai features authentic Thai cuisine with an extensive menu. Vegetarians will appreciate the fact that almost every menu item has tofu indicated as an option instead of meat. Lunch specials on weekdays. Try the Sweet Rice and Mango for dessert. The atmosphere features authentic Thai music and art. Service is very friendly and free parking is convenient.

Swagat Indian Cuisine

2074 NW Lovejoy • Portland • (503) 227-4300
See review – Beaverton

Sweet Basil Thai Cuisine

3135 NE Broadway St • Portland • (503) 281-8337

VegFriendly • Thai • Mon-Fri lunch • Daily dinner • Full service & take out
Entrees $5-10

The food here is well thought out and artfully presented using fresh ingredients. Let your server know you are vegetarian as tofu is an option on many dishes. Try their Lovely Ginger with Tofu or their House Special Curry. Be sure to specify your spicy tolerance: very mild to extremely wild. This charming converted bungalow features outdoor seating during warmer months. Reservations recommended due to space and popularity.

Sweet Lemon Vegetarian Bistro
4888 NW Bethany Blvd • Portland • (503) 617-1419
www.sweetlemonveggiebistro.com

Vegetarian • Asian • Mon-Sat lunch & dinner • Counter service & take out
Entrees $5-10

Located in the Bethany Village Centre on the west side of town, Sweet Lemon Vegetarian Bistro serves healthy and creative Asian dishes free of meat, eggs, and MSG. The counter service is friendly and the décor is colorful and casual. Menu items are elegantly presented and include wraps, salads, soups, and Sweet Lemon specials such as Zen Noodles and Eden Tofu. Brown rice and whole wheat tortillas are offered as options and organic ingredients are used when possible.

Taco Del Mar
3106 SE Hawthorne Blvd • Portland • (503) 232-7763 • www.tacodelmar.com
438 SE Martin Luther King Blvd • Portland • (503) 232-7695
736 SW Taylor • Portland • (503) 827-8311
12122 SE Division • Portland • (503) 761-3120
1930 SW 4th Ave • Portland • (503) 473 8660
9055-3 SW Barbur Blvd • Portland • (503) 244-0454
911 NW Hoyt St • Portland • (503) 274-4836
10215 NE Cascades Parkway • Portland • (503) 288-8795
See review – Beaverton

Thai Orchid Restaurant
2231 W Burnside St • Portland • (503) 226-4542 • www.thaiorchidrestaurant.com
10075 SW Barbur Blvd • Portland • (503) 452-2544
See review – Beaverton

Thanh Thai
4005 SE Hawthorne Blvd • Portland • (503) 238-6232

VegFriendly • Thai/Vietnamese • Lunch & dinner • Closed Tues • Full service & take out • Entrees $5-10

This popular restaurant located in the Hawthorne district serves seventeen vegetarian entrees including quite a few mock chicken dishes. For only $6-$7 an entree, you will get generous, filling portions. The atmosphere is casual and the service is fast.

The Tao of Tea

3430 SE Belmont St • Portland • (503) 736-0119

Vegetarian • International • Daily lunch & dinner • Full service • Entrees $5-10

Known primarily for their extensive tea varieties, this Asianesque tea house should not be overlooked as a place to dine as well. The completely vegetarian selection ranges from Indian to Japanese, with appetizers such as samosas and edamame. There are Greek, Lebanese, and Italian flatbreads, each with their own distinctive flavor and style. They also serve scrumptious desserts. With a soothing water fountain, tranquil background music, and walls adorned with eastern art, it offers a very relaxing atmosphere for an intimate meal.

Van Hanh

8446 SE Division St • Portland • (503) 788-0825 • www.vanhanhrestaurant.com

Vegetarian • Vietnamese • Tues-Sun lunch & dinner • Closed Mon • Entrees $5-$7

Vahn Hahn is a small, authentic but informal Vietnamese vegetarian restaurant operated by Buddhist nuns. The proceeds from the restaurant go to support a local monastery. All the food is made to order and the menu provides a pretty wide selection of dishes. Take out is also available. There is ample parking adjacent for this popular Portland vegetarian restaurant.

Veganopolis

412 SW 4th Ave • Portland • (503) 226-3400 • www.veganopolis.com

Vegan • American • Mon-Sat breakfast & lunch

Located right in the core downtown area of Portland, Veganopolis takes the healthy and delicious taste of vegan food to the mainstream. You order your meal on the lower level and then enjoy the urban ambience upstairs. Started by a couple of chefs originally from Chicago, this restaurant was opened by popular demand as more and more people asked for a chance to enjoy their great food. Something's lost in Chicago and something's found in Portland. Take this opportunity to add something special to the hustle and bustle of the city. You'll be glad you did.

Vege Thai

3274 SE Hawthorne • Portland • (503) 234-2171 • vegethai.com

Vegetarian • Thai • Daily lunch and dinner • Full service, take out, and catering
Entrées $5-10

Vege Thai was the first vegetarian restaurant in Portland and represents the new wave of vegetarian Thai cuisine: meatless, high in protein, no MSG, and no white sugar. Except for the eggs in a few dishes, every item on the menu is vegan or can be made vegan. No fish sauce, oyster sauce, or shrimp paste is used in any dish. Try Spicy "Chicken" with Basil, stir-fried soy chicken with garlic, chili, and basil leaves, or Pad Ki Mow, spicy rice noodles stir-fried with chili, basil leaves, and bamboo shoots. Black rice pudding with coconut milk or mango with sticky rice are two perfect ways to end a meal as healthy and delicious as the one you'll have at Vege Thai.

Vegetarian House
22 NW 4th Ave • Portland • (503) 274-0160; www.vegetarianhouse.com

Vegetarian • Chinese • Daily lunch and dinner • Full service & take out
Entrees $6-14

Situated near the main gate to Chinatown, Vegetarian House offers a vast, mostly vegan menu consisting primarily of mock meat dishes. Entrees include Veggie Sesame Chicken, Veggie Sweet and Sour Beef, and Veggie Fish with Brown Sauce. They have an all-you-can-eat weekday lunch buffet from 11am-2:30pm. The decor is casual and simple with an Asian flair, and the service is generally friendly and attentive.

Veggielicious
3315 SE Hawthorne Blvd • Portland • www.veggielicious.net

Vegan • Cart/American • Tues-Fri lunch & dinner • Sat & Sun lunch • Closed Mon
Entrees under $5 • Closed in Winter

This vegan food cart in the Hawthorne district offers veggie dogs and burgers, sandwiches and chili, as well as fresh juices and vegan cookies from Sweet Pea Bakery. Try the Grilled "Ham and Cheese" Sandwich, Hawaiian BBQ Tofu Sandwich, and the "Egg" Mock Muffin (weekends only). There are two stools available while you wait, but no tables for dining. Their products, which are made using organic tofu and local herbs and spices, can also be found at select stores around town.

Vita Café
3024 NE Alberta St • Portland • (503) 335-8233

VeryVegfriendly • American/International • Daily for three meals
Full service & take out • Entrees $5-10

Considered one of the most vegetarian/vegan friendly food spots in Portland, their menu includes such dishes as Vegan Chicken Fried Steak, Mushroom-Tempeh Paté, Vegan Lasagna and other dishes which range in cultural influence from American to Asian and Mediterranean to Mexican. Breakfast is served all day and includes such notable treats as Vegan Biscuits and Gravy, Vegan French Toast, and an array of different geographically categorized corn cakes. To top it all off, all of their breads and desserts are egg- and dairy-free. This restaurant is located in the Alberta Arts section of town and has an eclectic atmosphere.

Ya Hala
8005 SE Stark St • Portland • (503) 256-4484 • www.yahalarestaurant.com

VegFriendly • Lebanese • Mon-Sat for lunch and dinner • Full service & take out
Catering available • Entrees $8-12

Ya Hala Restaurant specializes in authentic Lebanese cuisine and offers many vegetarian options. Vegan dishes, which are clearly marked, include Artichoke Hearts, Makloube (eggplant casserole), and Veggie Mezza. Ya Hala's soups and stews are also entirely vegan. Fresh-baked, steaming pocket bread is brought to your table throughout the meal, so you will more than likely not go home hungry. Reservations are not accepted and you may therefore have to wait for a table at this popular restaurant. You can pass the time by stopping by the adjacent Mediterranean grocery store which features common Lebanese foods, ingredients, and spices.

SHOPPING

Alberta Cooperative Grocery

1500 NE Alberta St • Portland • (503) 287 4333 • www.albertagrocery.coop

A member-owned cooperative where all are welcome to shop. They carry natural foods and a wide variety of organic or sustainably grown produce. As a community resource, they provide information about food and other products. Neighbors meet here and a community bulletin board advertises neighborhood goods and services. Open daily 9am-10pm.

The Daily Grind

4026 SE Hawthorne • Portland • (503) 233-5521

This large store has been family owned for 15 years. Exceptional, all-organic fresh produce. Fresh salad bar. Fresh-made daily soups and casseroles for take out. Large bulk department, including bulk herbs. This is the only store in Portland stocking Loma Linda and Worthington foods. In-store bakery with fresh-made specialty breads, scones, muffins, etc. Extensive selection of quality vitamins and supplements. Open daily 9am-9pm.

Food Fight Grocery

1217 SE Stark St. • Portland • (503) 233-3910 • www.foodfightgrocery.com

"A vegan 7-11," this all-vegan convenience store carries mostly "junk food" and hard-to-find items, faux meats, frozen foods, T-shirts and comics. Vegan comfort food. One of a kind! Open daily 10am-8pm.

Food Front Co-op

2375 NW Thurman • Portland • (503) 222-5658 • www.foodfront.coop

Established over 30 years ago, this medium-to-large-sized store is conveniently located. It offers an excellent selection of local produce, bulk items, natural food items and non-food items. It has a vegetarian and vegan deli offering a fabulous selection of eclectic choices, snacks, coffee, pastries, juices, and fresh fruits. There's a small indoor/outdoor eating space. Open daily 8am-9pm.

New Seasons Market

5320 NE 33rd Ave • Portland • (503) 288-3838 • www.newseasonsmarket.com
7300 SW Beaverton-Hillsdale Hwy • Portland • (503) 292-6838
1214 SE Tacoma St • Portland • (503) 230-4949
1954 SE Division St. • Portland • (503) 445-2888
6400 N Interstate Ave • Portland • (503) 467-4777

Locally owned and operated grocery stores are fun, easy to shop and have everything you need—from thousands of natural and organic selections to the best of grocery basics. The bountiful produce department emphasizes organic and local products. In-store certified organic bakery offers 21 varieties of freshly baked organic bread and the delis make soups, salads, and entrees daily. Open daily 8am-10pm.

Organics to You

606 SE Madison St. • Portland • (503) 236-6496 • www.organicstoyou.org

Fresh, 100% certified organic produce and groceries, including breads, soy products, coffee, and dog treats, are delivered directly from local farmers and cooperatives to homes in Portland and most surrounding areas. A selection of different bin choices is offered.

People's Food Co-op

3029 SE 21st Ave • Portland • (503) 232-9051 • www.peoples.coop

An all-vegetarian (except pet food) natural foods co-op carrying a full line of fresh and packaged natural foods. Even the cheese is rennet-free. Vegan options as well as alternatives for allergies or nutritional preferences. Large selection of bulk food items. Fresh produce emphasizes seasonal organics purchased locally where possible. Bicycle delivery for area residents. Open daily 8am-10pm. Hosts a weekly farmers' market on Wednesdays, 2-7pm all year round.

Pioneer Organics

7911 NE 33rd • Portland • (503) 460-2729 • (877) 632-3424
www.pioneerorganics.com

Throughout the Portland area, Pioneer delivers various-sized boxes of fresh, certified organic fruits and vegetables to your door. They will also deliver a wide range of breads and groceries and welcome special orders.

Trader Joe's

2122 NW Glisan • Portland • (971) 544-0788 • www.traderjoes.com
4715 SE 39th Ave • Portland • (503) 777-1601
4121 NE Halsey St • Portland • (503) 284-1694

"TJ's" is a unique chain of medium-sized grocery stores often in tucked-away locations. You'll find a treasure of interesting products, mostly packaged, canned or bottled. There is a small but well-stocked fresh vegetable section and plenty of faux meats in the cooler or freezer. The kosher label will be found on an extensive number of products in virtually all categories. Many of the foods are private labeled with their own "angle," i.e., vegetarian, organic or just plain decadent. All have minimally processed ingredients from a variety of suppliers, many international, who make interesting products often exclusive to this chain. Known for generally low prices, there is a whole underground of wine aficionados who set price/value standards by TJ's bargain bottles. Open daily 9am-9pm.

Whole Foods Market

1210 NW Couch St • Portland • (503) 525-4343 • www.wholefoods.com

Located in the historic downtown Pearl District, this new store is designed to give urbanites the opportunity to celebrate quality-conscious natural foods, organic fruits and vegetables that are found in this local region. There is a good selection of faux meats and a selection of some of the world's best products. The staff is passionate about providing customers with a high standard of quality products and services, sharing information and educating. Open daily 8am-10pm.

Wild Oats Natural Marketplace

3535 NE 15th Ave • Portland • (503) 288-3414 • www.wildoats.com
2825 East Burnside St • Portland • (503) 232-6601

Now a part of the Whole Foods group, this attractive store offers a wide range of natural and organic foods, recycled paper products, fresh flowers, unique gift items and a large selection of supplements and body care items. There is a full service deli with vegetarian and vegan offerings. Open daily 9am-9pm.

FROM THE FARM

47th Avenue Farm

6632 SE 47th Avenue • (503) 777-4213 • www.47thAveFarm.com

An urban farm growing vegetables and herbs in Southeast Portland dedicated to growing produce for Portland residents, seasonally and sustainably based on a Community Supported Agriculture (CSA) model where the farm and families form a network of mutual support. Tuesday pick-up at the farm (see address above), bus accessible. Thursday pick-up in Lake Oswego at Luscher Farm, 125 Rosemont, West Linn. Summer and winter shares.

Alberta Farmers' Market

Last Thursday of Month, 5pm-7pm, End of May-September
NE 15th and Alberta
farmersmarket@albertagrocery.coop

Hillsdale Farmers' Market

Sundays, 10am-2pm, May-October
Wilson High School-Rieke Elementary Parking Lot, 1407 SW Vermont
www.hillsdalefarmersmarket.com

Hollywood Farmers' Market
Saturdays, 8am-1pm, May-October
Saturdays, 9am-1pm, November
NE Hancock between 44th & 45th, one block South of Sandy
www.hollywoodfarmersmarket.org

Interstate Farmers' Market
Wednesday, 3pm-7pm, Mid May-September
Overlook Park, N Fremont & Interstate
www.interstatefarmersmarket.com

Lents International Farmers' Market
Sunday, 9am-2pm, June-Mid October
Crossroads Plaza, SE 92nd and SE Foster

Lloyd Farmers' Market
Tuesday, 10am-2pm, Early July-September
NE Holladay St. between 7th and 9th

Montavilla Farmers' Market
Sundays, 10am-2pm, Mid July-September
SE 77th and SE Stark St.
www.montavillamarket.org

Moreland Farmers' Market
Wednesdays, 3:30pm-7:30pm, Mid May-September
SE Bybee and SE 14th St.
www.morelandfarmersmarket.org

OHSU Farmers' Market
Tuesdays, 1pm-5:30pm, Mid May-Early October
OHSU Auditorium Courtyard (near the fountain).

People's Farmers' Market
Wednesdays, 2pm-7pm, Year-round market
3029 SE 21st Avenue, one block north of Powell Blvd.
www.peoples.coop

Portland Farmers' Market – Eastbank
Thursdays, 3:30pm-7:30pm, Mid May-September
SE 20th, between Hawthorne and Belmont on Salmon Street
www.portlandfarmersmarket.org

Portland Farmers' Market – Portland State University
Saturdays, 8:30am-2pm, April-Mid December
Fall hours 9:30am-2pm, November-December

South Park Blocks between SW Montgomery and SW Harrison
www.portlandfarmersmarket.org

Portland Farmers' Market – Downtown
Wednesdays, 10am-2pm, May-October
South Park Blocks behind Schnitzer Concert Hall, SW Salmon & Park
www.portlandfarmersmarket.org

Portland Farmers' Market – EcoTrust
Thursdays evenings, 3:30pm-7:30pm, June-September
NW 10th between Irving & Johnson
www.portlandfarmersmarket.org

Sauvie Island Organics, LLC
20233 NW Sauvie Island Road • Portland • (503) 621-6921
www.sauvieislandorganics.com

SIO grows vegetables, herbs, salad mix, and flowers on an 18-acre farm located on the rich soils of Sauvie Island 20 minutes from downtown Portland. They cultivate 10 acres, specializing in a diversity of high quality fruits and vegetables for the fresh direct market. SIO sells primarily to local restaurants and has a 200-member CSA. They employ three full-time managers (field manager, restaurant/greens manager, crew leader) and offer a 17-month apprenticeship program to individuals with a serious interest in gaining the skills necessary to farm. Pick-up at Farm or in SE, NE or NW Portland.

RAINIER

Rainer Farmers' Market
Saturdays, 10am-3pm, Mid May-Early September
Riverfront Park on "A" Street
www.rainier97048.org

SCAPPOOSE

Scappoose Community Club Farmers' Market
Saturdays, 9am-2pm, Mid May-Mid September
1st & E. Columbia Ave
www.scappoosefarmermarket.com

SEASIDE

Seaside Health Foods
144 N Roosevelt • Seaside • (503) 738 3088

Offers a plentiful selection of packaged, frozen, and refrigerated foods suitable for vegetarians and vegans. They carry a large variety of bulk herbs and foods, teas, snacks, books and beauty aids. An added bonus is the juice bar and fresh organic produce case. Helpful staff will research information and accommodate special orders. Open Mon-Fri 9:30am-5:30pm, Sat 9:30am-5pm, closed Sun.

SHERWOOD

Taco Del Mar
21155 SW Baler Way • Sherwood • (503) 625-3967 • www.tacodelmar.com
See review – Beaverton

Sherwood Saturday Market
Saturdays, 9am-1pm, May-September
City of Sherwood City Hall
www.sherwoodmarket.blogspot.com

TIGARD

DINING

Sweet Tomatoes
6600 SW Cardinal Lane • Tigard • (503) 443-6161 • www.sweettomatoes.com
See review – Beaverton

SHOPPING

Whole Foods Market
7380 SW Bridgeport Road • Tigard • (503) 639-6500
See description – Portland

FROM THE FARM

Tigard Area Farmers' Market
Sundays, 9am-2pm, Mid May-October
Washington Square Too Parking Lot on Greenburg Road
www.tigardfarmersmarket.com

TILLAMOOK

Tillamook Farmers' Market
Saturdays, 9am-2pm, Mid June-September
2nd and Laurel Ave
www.tillamookfarmersmarket.com

TROUTDALE

DINING

Taco Del Mar
2705 NE 238th Drive • Troutdale • (503) 661 4344 • www.tacodelmar.com
See review – Beaverton

FROM THE FARM

Bumblebee Farm
30006 SE Division Dr • Troutdale • (503) 704-0775

A certified organic family farm specializing in great-tasting, healthy varieties of vegetables straight from the fields to the table   Their CSA provides vegetables, herbs,
flowers, and fruit June through November. Bumblebee Farm believes that by simply
growing great food and selling locally that they help to create a healthy synergy of
cooperation and inspiration between the producer and the informed consumer.
Bumblebee Farm is proud to be helping an important effort in Portland to link
farm-fresh food to local area schools.

Dancing Roots Farm
29820 E Woodard Rd • Troutdale • (503) 695-3445 • www.dancingrootsfarm.com

"Part of the Solution" is what this small family business seeks to be by offering high
quality, fresh produce for a number of local restaurants as well as individuals and
households through their farm membership (or CSA) program. They grow over 100
varieties of vegetables, herbs, fruit, and flowers all chosen for their flavor, nutrition, genetic diversity, and beauty. Their season is 26 weeks long, mid-May through
Thanksgiving.

Troutdale Farmers' and Artists' Market
Saturday, 10am-3pm, April-Mid November
Holiday Market: 4th Fri Nov-4th Sat Dec 10am-3pm (indoor venue)
Historic Troutdale Railroad Depot, 473 E. Historic Columbia River Hwy
www.windancefarmsandart.com

TUALATIN

Taco Del Mar
18747 SW Martinazzi Ave • Tualatin • (503) 691 9695 • www.tacodelmar.com
See review – Beaverton

WEST LINN

DINING

Taco Del Mar
22000 Willamette Dr • West Linn • (503) 594-0511 • www.tacodelmar.com
See review – Beaverton

Thai Orchid Restaurant
18740 Willamette Dr • West Linn • (503) 699-4195
www.thaiorchidrestaurant.com
See review – Beaverton

FROM THE FARM

West Linn Farmers' Market
Wednesday, 4:30pm-8:30pm, Mid May-September
1725 Willamette Falls Drive
www.westlinnchamber.com/FarmerArtistMarket

WILSONVILLE

Taco Del Mar
8593 SW Main St • Wilsonville • (503) 582-8226 • www.tacodelmar.com
See review – Beaverton

YAMHILL

Gaining Ground Farm
21480 NE Laughlin Rd. • Yamhill • (971) 275-2842
www.gaininggroundfarm.com

A community-supported farm dedicated to providing healthy, local, fresh food and
reconnecting people with what they eat. The core business is focused on selling
directly to consumers. They want their customers to know the farm and where their
food comes from as much as they enjoy the vegetables, herbs, and flowers the farm
grows. Their CSA provides a weekly share of the farm's harvest over a 20 week
season with a box of fresh, local, delicious vegetables coming straight from the farm
to the table, June through October.

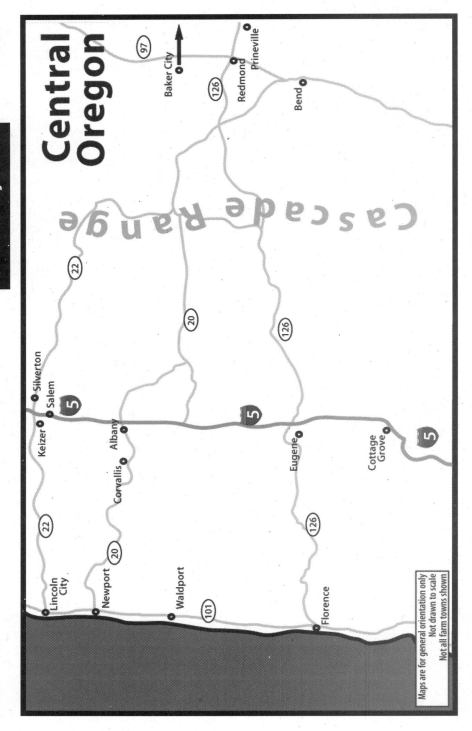

Central Oregon

Cascade Range

97 · Baker City

126 · Redmond · Prineville

Bend

22

20

126

Silverton
Salem
Keizer
5
Albany
Corvallis
5
Eugene
Cottage Grove
5

22
20
126
Lincoln City
Newport
Waldport
101
Florence

Maps are for general orientation only
Not drawn to scale
Not all farm towns shown

Central Oregon

ALBANY

Albany Farmers' Market
Saturdays, 9am-1pm, Mid April-Late November
4th & Ellsworth (City Hall Parking Lot)
www.locallygrown.org

BAKER CITY

Baker City Farmers' Market
Saturdays, 10am-12 noon, End of June-September
Geiser-Pollman Park at Campbell and Grove St.

BEND

DINING

Café Yumm
325 SW Powerhouse Drive • Bend • (541) 318-9866 • www.cafeyumm.com
See review – Eugene

Taco Del Mar
63455 N Hwy 97 • Bend • (541) 317-1112
320 SW Century Drive • Bend • Opening soon • www.tacodelmar.com
See review – Beaverton

SHOPPING

Devore's Good Food Store
1124 NW Newport Ave • Bend • (541) 389-6588

A locally-owned store and deli for over 27 years featuring all-organic produce, natural and ethnic groceries, fine wines and micro-brews. The deli has incredible take out foods including soups, salads, meat analogs, wraps, dips, and desserts, all with vegetarian or vegan options. Open Mon-Sat 8am-7pm, Sun 9am-6pm.

Trader Joe's
63455 North Highway 97 • Bend • Opening soon
See description – Portland

Wild Oats Natural Marketplace
2610 NE Hwy 20 • Bend • (541) 389-0151 • www.wildoats.com
See description – Portland

FROM THE FARM

Bend Farmers' Market
Wednesdays, 3pm-7pm, June-October
Top of Mirror Pond Park off Franklin Blvd

Fridays, 2pm-6pm, June-Mid October
St. Charles Medical Center • 2500 East Neff Road
bendfarmersmkt@bendbroadband.com

Fields Farms
61915 Petteygrew Road • Bend • (541) 382-8059

Fields farm is a small family farm offering organic vegetables from the beginning of June through the end of October. They have a CSA of 50-60 members, participate in the local farmers' market and sell direct from the farm. Crops grow at this high elevation are particularly sweet and tender. One farm internship position is available yearly.

BLACHLY

Horton Road Organics
93851 Horton Rd • Blachly • (541) 925-3019 • www.hortonorganics.com

This five-acre market garden, located in the Oregon Coast Range, specializes in carefully cultivated fresh organic vegetables and an educational program for aspiring farmers. They grow 34 different organic vegetable crops from April through November specializing in selective cool season plants that suit their mountain climate including "luscious greens, rich brassicas, and sweet roots." This 14-year-old CSA has 110 members who, in addition to vegetables, also receive newsletters, recipes, email, and discounts at the Farmers' Market stand.

BROWNSVILLE

Brownsville Co-op Farmers' Market
Saturdays, 9am-1pm, End of April-Late November
260 North Main St
www.brownsvillecoop.com

CORVALLIS

DINING

China Blue
2307 NW 9th St • Corvallis • (541) 757-8088

VeryVegFriendly • Chinese • Daily lunch and dinner • Full service, catering, and take out • Entrées $5-10

"Eat healthy, be happy" is the very apt motto for China Blue. The menu is impressively long, with most items available in vegetarian and vegan versions with tofu, tempeh, and seitan options. Health-conscious choices also include wheat-free cuisine and recipes based on American Heart Association recommendations. MSG- and transfat-free dishes like Cantonese Chow Yuk, with Chinese cabbage and seitan, Szechuan tempeh, and gourmet fusion Hazelnut tofu will convince you that healthy eating can indeed bring much happiness.

China Delight
325 NW 2nd St • Corvallis • (541) 753-3753

VegFriendly • Chinese • Open daily for lunch and dinner • Full service & take out
Entrees $5-10

Healthy, delicious vegetarian entrees including their famously addictive sesame tempeh. The service and atmosphere is friendly, and almost all of their dishes have a vegetarian option. Meal choices go beyond your typical fare to items such as vegetarian "pork chop," tofu with rosemary, and Da Vinci tofu.

Evergreen Indian Cuisine
136 SW 3rd St • Corvallis • (541) 754-7944 • evergreenindianrestaurant.com

VeryVegFriendly • Indian • Daily lunch and dinner • Full service, buffet, and take out • Entrées $10-20

One of the most popular restaurants in downtown Corvallis, Evergreen has many good vegetarian options and many dishes can be made vegan upon request. Entrées are served either a la carte, with rice and naan, or as Thali dinners, with a main entrée, vegetable curry of the day, dal, sambar (soup), raita, rice, naan, papadum, and dessert of the day. Vegans should ask for roti instead of naan. Try any of the vegetable pakoras or the vegetable samosa as appetizers. Try the vegetable karai, mixed vegetables cooked with tomatoes, onions, and bell pepper in a special sauce, or the Evergreen combo, a southern Indian specialty with masala dosa, for interesting new taste experiences.

Feast Alternative (in First Alternative Co-op)
1007 SE 3rd St • Corvallis • (541) 753-3115 • www.firstalt.coop

VegFriendly • Deli • Daily 9am-9pm

This co-op makes delicious dishes for their deli. All ingredients are organic and local whenever possible. Easy meals such as torte verde and caramelized onion lasagna, salad bar, fresh made-to-order sandwiches, hot pizza, and soups. Fresh vegan and vegetarian bakery items daily. Indoor and outdoor seating available. Full details of ingredients are helpful.

Nearly Normal's

109 NW 15th St • Corvallis • (541) 753-0791

Vegetarian • International • Mon-Sat, all three meals • Closed Sun • Full service & take out • Entrees $5-10

Affectionately called "Gonzo Cuisine," from vegan breakfast burritos to gonzo pad thai or "tempehchangas" to BBQ tempeh burgers, there is not a customary plate on the menu. The organic soups, salads and daily specials are each their own exceptional, unique meal. This funky yet classy restaurant supports a thoughtfulness in preparation and presentation of food, where original vegetarian recipes are invented behind the counter, born from "creative chaos."

Señor Sam's

140 NW 3rd St • Corvallis • (541) 754-7448

VeryVegFriendly • Mexican • Daily lunch and dinner • Cafeteria and take-out Entrées $5-10

Bring a big appetite to Señor Sam's. While the décor is plain, there are sixteen generously-sized vegetarian options on the menu, all of them $6.75 or less. Besides the usual taco salad and burritos, there's the vegetarian chimichanga and veggie fajita burrito with sauteed peppers, onions, and tomatoes. Vegans can ask for theirs without cheese or guacamole (which has sour cream). Señor Sam's also has a frequent buyer card: buy 12 meals and get one free!

Taco Del Mar

1915 NW 9th St • Corvallis • (541) 738-0540 • www.tacodelmar.com
See review – Beaverton

Tarntip Thai Cuisine

2535 NW Monroe St • Corvallis • (541) 757-8906

VeryVegFriendly • Thai • Mon-Sat lunch & dinner • Sun dinner only • Full service and take out • Entrées $5-10

Located across the street from Oregon State University, Tarntip is a busy Thai restaurant, popular with students and townspeople alike. With several vegetarian appetizers and soups, a vegetarian menu, and 16 other entrées that are readily converted for vegans and vegetarians, Tarntip is a good choice for a tasty night on the town. Try Mixed Vegetable Curry in coconut milk with tofu for a slightly sweet spicy treat, or for something really different, try Paht Ma Moung Him Ma Parn, that is, cashew nuts, onion, bell pepper, and carrot with black curry sauce.

SHOPPING

First Alternative Co-op

1007 SE 3rd St • Corvallis • (541) 753-3115 • www.firstalt.coop
2855 NW Grant Ave • Corvallis • (541) 452-3115

Both stores offer a large variety of natural, organic foods, body care products, supplements and general merchandise. Options for vegans, vegetarians and people with allergies and special diet requirements. The kitchen makes delicious dishes for their Feast Alternative deli. Easy meals and salad bar with indoor and outdoor seating at the 3rd St store. Open daily 9am-9pm.

FROM THE FARM

Corvallis Farmers' Market
Wednesdays, 8am-1pm, Mid April-Late November
110 SW 53rd St

Saturdays, 9am-1pm, Mid April-Late November
1st & Jackson (North end of riverfront)
www.locallygrown.org

Indoor Winter Farmers' Market
2nd and 4th Saturdays, 9am-1pm, January-March
Guerber Hall, Benton County Fairgrounds, 110 SW 53rd St
www.gatheringtogetherfarm.com/wintermarket.html

CRESWELL

Sweetwater Farm & Nursery
83036 Weiss Rd • Creswell • (541) 895-3431 • www.goodfoodeasy.com

A 20-acre organic farm established in 1979 producing mushrooms and over 50 types of vegetables & berries. There is a choice of 3 sizes of CSA boxes to fit any family with a 4-week commitment at a time. Items from other local organic farms may be included in the off season to keep an interesting mix year around. Weekly newsletters with recipes.

EUGENE

DINING

Café Yumm!
730 E Broadway • Eugene • (541) 344-9866 • www.cafeyumm.com
1005 Green Acres Rd • Eugene • (541) 684-9866
130 Oakway Center • Eugene • (541) 465-9866
1801 Willamette St • Eugene • (541) 686-9866

Vegetarian • American/International • Daily for three meals • Full service & take out • Entrees $5-10

Based around their signature sauces, they have developed a distinctive style of healthy, sustainable vegetarian meals. Rice and beans have never been prepared in so many delicious ways on a single menu. You can choose between the likes of a

·Yumm! wrap with tofu, or a Chilean zucchini corn stew and rice dish. Great care is given to the quality of the recipes and ingredients which highlight sustainable, organic and truly Yummy! meals. Soups, salads, and finger foods are also offered, as well as their sauces and marinades.

Cosmic Pizza

199 W 8th • Eugene • (541) 338-9333 • www.cozmicpizza.com

VeryVegFriendly • Pizza • Open daily • Take out or order in with free delivery in an electric vehicle

A pleasant organic pizzeria with a heart. Create your pizza with vegetarian Canadian bacon or pepperoni or just go for a choice of organic vegetable toppings and add cheezy tofu topping. This all goes on a gluten-free crust made from potato and rice flour. Owner Joel encourages folks to bring a board game and stay for the evening. Locals will order Genesis Juice, Rusty's Handbuilt Cookies, and vegan cheeszecake.

Evergreen Indian Cuisine

1525 Franklin Blvd • Eugene • (541) 343-7944 • evergreenindianrestaurant.com
See review – Corvallis

Holy Cow Café

1222 E 13th Ave at U of O Student Union • Eugene • (541) 346-2562
www.holycowcafe.com

Vegetarian • Café • Phone for hours • Closed Sat-Sun

Organic vegetarian gourmet food at affordable prices. Ethnic comfort food from around the world, plus an organic salad bar and grab-and-go selections, fair trade teas, and homemade soups and breads. Family owned to provide right livelihood by offering healthy international comestibles low on the food chain. Great taste. Lively ambience in a college setting.

Keystone Café

395 West 5th Ave • Eugene • (541) 342-2075

Vegetarian • American/International • Daily for breakfast & lunch • Full service Entrees $5-10

This popular hangout boasts a uniquely Eugene décor and menu centered on an impressive array of vegetarian breakfast items which are served all day. Keystone also offers a creatively thought out selection of vegan dishes. Reasonable prices and well-prepared organic meals are a few of the reasons why Keystone is repeatedly voted one of Eugene's favorite vegetarian restaurants. Try the vegan French toast or the vegan power breakfast to find out why everyone loves this neighborhood mainstay.

Lotus Garden

810 Charnelton Ave • Eugene • (541) 344-1928

Vegan • Chinese • Lunch & dinner • Closed Tues & Sun

Founded by a Taoist practitioner serving a variety of delicious, high-protein, faux-meat dishes as well as a great many vegetable dishes. The most popular are reported to be Hunan veggie beef, spring rolls, pot stickers, wonton soup, mushu "pork," and the veggie shrimp dishes.

Manola's Thai Cuisine

652 E Broadway • Eugene • (541) 342-6666 • www.manolasthai.com

VeryVegFriendly • Thai • Daily lunch and dinner • Full service and delivery
Entrées $5-10

Manola's offers a two-page vegetarian and vegan menu with many innovative and tasty dishes you may not have seen elsewhere, such as seaweed soup, made with fresh ginger, seaweed, green onions, mushrooms, cabbage, tofu, glass noodles, celery, and roasted garlic. Som Tum, one of the four vegetarian salads, is a spicy green papaya salad with tomatoes, fresh garlic, green beans, roasted peanuts, carrots, lime juice, and sticky rice. Make sure to try the fresh ginger iced tea, and leave room for the golden-fried banana or banana rolls for dessert.

Morning Glory Bakery & Café & Out of the Fog Coffeehouse

450 Willamette St • Eugene • (541) 687-0709

Vegetarian • Café & Coffeehouse • Daily for breakfast & lunch

A happy combination where the socially and earth-conscious gather to share thoughts on important issues, have a vegetarian breakfast or lunch (vegan on request) and sip socially responsible organic shade-grown Café Mom coffee. The eclectic menu features delicious tofu scramble with soysage, Tofu Luna sandwich, Triple Lucky Noodle dish, homemade flatbread and vegan baked goods and much more.

New Day Bakery & Café

449 Blair Blvd • Eugene • (541) 345-1695

VegFriendly • Bakery & Café • Daily for three meals • Full service & take out
Entrees $5-10

This little bakery in the heart of Eugene's cultural hub serves a wide variety of cheap meals. From tofu scrambles and veggie fajitas to tempeh sandwiches and vegetarian tamales, New Day Bakery serves more than just excellent bakery items. Fast, friendly counter service, generous veggie options, and an eclectic atmosphere make this café a great choice for any meal.

New Odyssey Juice & Java

1004 Willamette St • Eugene • (541) 484-7411 • www.newodyssey.us

Vegetarian • Open Mon-Sat for three meals • Sun lunch only • Entrees all under $5

An energetic center for fresh-squeezed organic raw juices and smoothies and/or organic free-trade, shade-grown Café Mom coffee. Enjoy daily meal specials. Most food can be prepared vegan. Their soy sirloin has converted many. One of the biggest sellers is the BLT made with hickory-smoked tofu. Many Mexican-style options, also quiches, lasagnes and mock shepherd's pies. They enthusiastically support Performance Art, in particular electronic computer music, much of which is created and performed with laptops on premises.

Ratatouille Bistro-Cafe
1530 Willamette Street • Eugene • (541) 344-0203 • www.ratatouillebistro.com

Vegetarian • Northwest Organic in a French style • Wed-Sun for lunch & dinner Closed Mon-Tues • Entrees $10-20

Ratatouille Bistro-Cafe is an exciting and new restaurant featuring 100 percent organic Northwest vegetarian cuisine served in a French atmosphere. Imagine you're in Paris around 1949. You turn down a side street and there is a lovely bistro. You go inside. Try the roasted sweet dumpling squash for dinner. For brunch try the breakfast burrito. Don't forget to see the menu of organic wines. The desserts are very creative. Anyone for chocolate pumpkin cake filled with hazelnut ganache and drizzled with coffee cinnamon sauce? The service is friendly and there are many vegan options. Bon appétit!

Sam Bond's Garage
407 Blair • Eugene • (541) 431-6603

Vegetarian • Pub grub • Daily 4pm-late

Eat, drink, breathe, and dance. Pizza by the slice, appetizers, soups, salads, along with great micro-brews, juice, and soft drinks. Kids welcome till 8:30pm. Entertainment nightly.

Sundance Salad Bar & Hot Buffet (in Sundance Natural Foods)
748 E 24th at Hilyard • Eugene • (541) 343-9142

Vegetarian • Breakfast, lunch & dinner • Open daily

A traditional natural food store that also offers a self-service salad bar and hot buffet with many imaginative vegan and vegetarian hot dishes. Reported to be the "best deli for a vegan meal anywhere around." There are vegan offerings daily and vegetarian pizzas. Restaurant quality food at deli prices.

Sweet Life Patisserie
755 Monroe St • Eugene • (541) 683-5676

Vegan • Patisserie • Open daily

A beautiful dessert café known and loved by vegans especially for the vegan "cheeze" cake and vegan chocolate cake. Products are gluten- and margarine-free and made from scratch with organically grown ingredients where possible. The place to go for thoughtful wedding and birthday cakes.

Taco Del Mar
3007 North Delta Hwy • Eugene • (541) 434-8226 • www.tacodelmar.com
See review – Beaverton

Toby's Tofu Palace
At the Eugene Saturday Market and area street & country fairs and music festivals
No phone, just be there.

This is a booth which has reappeared at Saturday Market for decades because folks have always flocked there for its unusually appealing foods such as the Tofu Tia, an especially scrumptious taco with tofu, sprouts, and a secret red sauce which can be expanded to the Tia Special with the addition of avocado, onions, and vegan sour cream. One unique product is Toby's Tofu Paté, which makes a fabulous eggless egg salad sandwich. Finish off with a blueberry tofu "cheesecake" washed down with the Palace Cooler. As for the specific address, just follow the crowds. It wouldn't be Saturday Market without Toby's.

Three Forks Wok & Grill
2560 Willamette St • Eugene • (541) 485-8489

VeryVegFriendly • Northwest and Pan-Asian • Lunch and dinner • Full service and take out • Entrées $5-10

Located in a small shopping mall, Three Forks is a locally owned and operated restaurant that uses the freshest local ingredients and lets customers choose the combinations and flavors they want. The menu offers a variety of made-to-order options. Menu items are vegan and prepared on vegan woks and pans unless meat is added to the entrée. Take your choice of tofu or tempeh, then choose wok, grill, salad, or all three, tempura vegetables or a sandwich on a tasty onion bun, and mango sorbet to create your own perfect lunch or dinner.

SHOPPING

Friendly Street Market
2757 Friendly St • Eugene • (541) 683-2079

A small, locally owned and operated neighborhood natural food store featuring local, seasonal and organic foods including a wide variety of vegetarian, vegan and specialty packaged and frozen foods as well as health and beauty aids, gifts, beer and wine. Open Mon-Sat 8am-10pm, Sun 9am-10pm.

Sundance Natural Market
748 E 24th Ave • Eugene • (541) 343-9142

A well-organized friendly market with a great selection of local, 100% organic produce, a nice bulk foods section and a great organic vegetarian deli featuring a hot food buffet, green and prepared salad bar, grab-and-go items, and pastries. There are vegan offerings daily and vegetarian pizzas. Restaurant-quality food at deli prices. Open daily 7am-11pm.

Trader Joe's
85 Oakway Center • Eugene • (541) 485-1744 • www.traderjoes.com
See review – Portland

Wild Oats Natural Marketplace
2580 Willakenzie Rd • Eugene • (541) 334-6382 • www.wildoats.com
2489 Willamette St • Eugene • (541) 345-1014
See description – Portland

FROM THE FARM

Hand To Mouth Organics
91 Alberta Lane • Eugene • (541) 461-6642

This two-acre farm is off River Road, just north of Eugene. It has been providing boxes offer generous proportions, wide variety, fabulously flavored produce on a week-by-week basis to its CSA members.

FOOD for Lane County's Youth Farm
FFLC 770 Bailey Hill Road • Eugene • (541) 343-2822

An urban 3-acre educational farm in Springfield where youth gain leadership skills, nutrition awareness, and work experience while serving their community growing produce for distribution to low-income households through FOOD for Lane County. Teens assist in tending the farm, managing the onsite farm stand, and preparing CSA boxes. The program welcomes tours and volunteers.

Full Circle Community Farm
1225 E Beacon Dr • Eugene • (541) 461-3798.

A biodynamic farm since 1997, they bicycle-deliver vegetables, fruit, and flowers to town for CSA members. They offer on-farm pickup to neighbors. Education experiences for members and School District 4J students, open house days, member workday potlucks, and the Pumpkin Parade. Visits are welcome.

Lane County (Eugene) Farmers' Market
Tuesdays, 10am-3pm, May-October
Saturdays, 9am-4pm, April-Mid November
East 8th & Oak St

Thursdays, 2pm-7pm, June-September
Lane County Fairgrounds, Admin Parking Lot, West 13th and Monroe St
www.lanecountyfarmersmarket.com

NettleEdge Farm Winter CSA
1640 Beacon Dr • Eugene • (541) 689-3672 • November-April

Located a Eugene's northern edge, Nettle Edge works "...to reconnect our neighbors and members to small scale farming and the benefit of locally produced foods on our winter diets." Winter sign-up begins in June.

FLORENCE

Salmonberry Naturals
812 Quince St • Florence • (541) 997-3345 • www.salmonberrynaturals.com

Small and well-stocked country store in business for 12 years. Friendly and knowledgeable staff. Focus on local and organic foods. Over 300 bulk herbs and spices and over 250 bulk food, nuts, seeds, and dried fruits. Some raw food items available. Mon-Fri 9:30am-6pm, Sat 9:30am-5:30pm, Sun 1pm-5pm.

INDEPENDENCE

Independence Farmers' Market
Saturdays, 9am-1pm, April-Mid November
Sterling Bank South, 302 Main Street

JUNCTION CITY

Groundwork Organic Farm
30699 Maple Drive • Junction City • (541) 998-0900

Fifty certified-organic acres 10 miles north of Eugene growing a wide variety of fruits and vegetables for sale at seven farmers' markets every week. The CSA program is in its 5th season running from May through October. Extended season shares are also available, October through December.

KEIZER

Taco Del Mar
6375 Ulali Drive • Keizer • (503) 390-1267 • www.tacodelmar.com
See review – Beaverton

KINGS VALLEY

Kings Valley Farmers' Market
Sundays, 1pm-4pm, June-Early October
Corner of Hwy 223 & Maxfield Creek Rd

DINING

Andaman Thai Cuisine

660 SE Highway 101 • Lincoln City • (541) 996-8424

VegFriendly • Thai • Daily lunch and dinner • Full service and take out
Entrées $5-10

Located in a small shopping mall off Highway 101, Andaman Thai Cuisine offers several vegetarian and vegan options with spice levels from "mild" to "extremely wild." Try "Fresh Wrapped" for an appetizer, rice paper wrapped with veggies, tofu, sweet basil and mint, served with peanut sauce, or Special House Curry, with tofu, red curry peanut sauce with bell pepper, carrots, and broccoli. And then there's "I Love Veggies," stir-fried mixed vegetables and tofu in the house special sauce.

Avanti Italian Cuisine

3521 SW Highway 101 • Lincoln City • (541) 902-3192 • www.ccarts.com/avanti

VegFriendly • Italian • Daily dinner • Full service and take out • Entrées $10-20
Closed Sun-Mon.

Located across the highway from Theatre West, Avanti combines Old World charm and southern Italian flavors with ocean-view dining. There are a number of traditional vegetarian choices such as tortellini, ravioli, and eggplant parmigiana. Vegan options include several types of pasta with a choice of sauteed vegetable sauces or marinara sauce.

Jasmine Thai Restaurant

1473 NW Highway 101 • Lincoln City • (541) 994-2022

VeryVegFriendly • Thai • Daily lunch and dinner • Full service and take out
Entrées $5-10

Conveniently located on Highway 101, Jasmine Thai Restaurant offers a menu of 101 authentic Thai dishes, with more than half of them available for vegetarians and vegans. Try salad rolls with Hoisin sauce or tofu satay as appetizers and, if you're brave enough, Evil Jungle Prince, red curry with broccoli, cabbage, mushrooms, basil, and tempeh or tofu.

SHOPPING

Trillium Natural Foods

1026 SE Jetty Ave • Lincoln City • (541) 994-5665

Trillium's primary focus is fresh, organically grown whole foods. It is a small store yet has one of the best selections on the Oregon coast, including a large bulk products section. Prices are good, too. Mon-Sat 9:30am-7pm, Sun 11am-5pm.

FROM THE FARM

Lincoln City Farmers' Market
Sundays, 9am-2pm, June-September
540 NE Hwy 101, De Lake School
www.lincolncityfarmersmarket.org

LORANE

Hey Bayles Farm
25766 Siuslaw River Rd • Lorane • (541) 767-0379 • www.heybaylesfarm.com

Certified organic produce comes direct from farmer to consumer for those in the CSA program. The farm specializes in garden varieties sought after by discriminating restaurants and rarely provided by growers

MADRAS

Madras Saturday Market
Saturdays, 9am-2pm, June-September
Sahalee Park, 7th & C Street

NEWPORT

DINING

Oceana Natural Foods Cooperative
159 SE 2nd St • Newport • (541) 265 8285 • www.oceanafoods.org

VeryVegFriendly • Deli • Open Mon. – Fri. 11am to 5pm

The smell of soup entices you in when you come in the store. There is a pleasant sit-down eating area where a wide range of food choices are available, including vegan, wheat-free, dairy-free, and sugar-free items. Organic ingredients are used whenever possible.

SHOPPING

Oceana Natural Foods Cooperative
159 SE 2nd St • Newport • (541) 265-3893 • www.oceanafoods.org

The emphasis is organic products from bulk foods to wine, beer, spices and herbs, cheese and other dairy products. They carry organic socks(!), organic coffee, tea, tortillas, meat, juice, and chips. The friendly staff can assist with information on dietary needs, supplements and other health related subjects. There is a pleasant sit-down eating area where a wide range of food choices is available including vegan, wheat-free, dairy-free and sugar-free items. Open Mon-Fri 8am-7pm, Sat 8am-6pm, Sun 10am-6pm.

FROM THE FARM

Newport Saturday Farmers' Market
Saturdays, 9am-1pm, May-October
Hwy 101 & Alder St, 1/2 mile N from Yaquina Bay Bridge
www.newportfarmersmarket.org

NOTI

Winter Green Community Farm
89762 Poodle Creek Rd • Noti • (541) 935-1920 • www.wintergreenfarm.com

Over 15 years offering weekly CSA boxes of organic produce fresh from the farm. This two-family farm in the foothills of the Coast Range 20 miles west of Eugene grows over 40 different fruits & vegetables. On-farm events with hay rides, garlic braiding, and scarecrow making. 19- or 24-week season. Pickup sites are in area neighborhoods.

PHILOMATH

Gathering Together Farm
25159 Grange Hall Road • Philomath • (541) 929-4289
www.gatheringtogetherfarm.com

The farm, which began in 1987, is a project in certified-organic vegetable and fruit production. They farm about 50 acres but all the fields are small, odd-shaped parcels of land 1 to 5 acres in size hugging Mary's River. In the heat of the summer there can be over 40 people working feverishly to produce high-quality food and get it directly to market. They have a roadside farm stand for seasonal organic vegetables and serve unforgettable lunches Saturday breakfast as well as a farm brunch on the 1st and 3rd Sundays of the month.

PRINEVILLE

Prineville Farmers' Market
Saturdays, 9am-12 noon, June-Mid October
Prineville City Plaza, across from Courthouse

REDMOND

Redmond Farmers' Market
Mondays, 2pm-6pm, Memorial Day-Labor Day
St. Charles Medical Center, off Kingwood Ave
www.redmondfarmersmarket.com

RICKREALL

Polk County Farmers' Market
Sundays, 9am-3pm, May-Mid November
Rickreall Grange Hall (School), 280 Hwy 99W

SALEM

DINING

Kwan's Original Cuisine
835 Commercial St SE • Salem • (503) 362-7711 • www.kwanscuisine.com

VeryVegFriendly • Chinese • Daily lunch & dinner • Full service & take-out

Kwan's features authentic Chinese cuisine with extensive vegetarian options. This restaurant goes the extra mile with a custom filtered-water system and a large viewing window looking into the kitchen so that diners can see that nothing is left to chance. The chef, originally from Hong Kong, brings his special knowledge and skills that are sure to delight Northwest diners. Convenient parking and a take out menu round out this little gem in Salem.

Marco Polo Global Restaurant
210 Liberty St SE • Salem • (503) 364-4833 • www.mpologlobal.com

VeryVegFriendly • Chinese, European-American • Daily lunch and dinner • Full service, buffet, take out, and catering • Entrées $5-10 • Closed Sun.

Located in the heart of downtown Salem, Marco Polo Global Restaurant is a welcome find for travelers in Oregon's mid-valley region. Owned by a family with two vegetarian members, Marco Polo has a menu that will delight vegetarians and vegans alike with over 70 items to choose from. European-American specialties include North American Tofu, House Pesto Salad, and Veggie Raspberry Pistachio "Chicken," all vegan. Marco Polo brings together the best of East and West in all of their menu options, so everyone in the family can be happy.

Thai Orchid Restaurant
285 Liberty St NE, Salem • (503) 391-2930 • www.thaiorchidrestaurant.com
See review – Beaverton

SHOPPING

LifeSource Natural Foods
2649 Commercial St SE • Salem • (503) 361-7973
www.lifesourcenaturalfoods.com

LifeSource is Salem's largest natural foods store and a welcome oasis of natural, organic, vegetarian, and vegan products. The staff is knowledgeable and enthusiastic about natural foods, environmental sustainability, and the building of community. They offer a full range of bulk foods, fair-trade and local items, organic produce, a good range of vegan and vegetarian groceries, and nutritional supplements and personal care items. The Deli, Salad & Hot Food bar offers entrées such as Indonesian Vegetables, Mushroom Stroganoff, Fried Happy "Chicken," Walnut Loaf, and Garden Vegetable Lasagna. Open Mon-Sat 8am-9pm, Sun 9am-8pm.

FROM THE FARM

Salem Farmers' Market
Wednesday, 10am-3pm, May-October
Chemeketa St NE between Commercial & High St. NE

Saturdays, 9am-3pm, May-October
Summer St & Marion St NE, Green State Parking Lot

Saturdays, 8:30am-1pm, Year-round, heated indoor market
1240 Rural Ave SE
www.salemsaturdaymarket.com

Whistling Frog Farm
3610 Oak Knoll Rd NW • Salem • (503) 763-0984

A small, sustainable family-run farm specializing in naturally grown produce with the minimal use of machines, no pesticides, no herbicides, no hormones or antibiotics, and selling produce only locally. Many of their vegetables are heirloom varieties. These seeds have not been subjected to hybridizing and still have the same great taste that has kept them around for many years. Through their CSA they sell grains, beans, fruits, vegetables, and herbs.

SILVERTON

Silverton Farmers' Market
Saturdays, 9am-1pm, Mid May-Mid October
Town Square Park, Main & Fiske

WALDPORT

Natural Selection
145 NW Hwy 101 • Waldport • (541) 563-6101

With many of a vegetarian or vegan's favorite products, this store is a great place to stop on your way along Highway 101 to pick up supplies for a picnic, goodies for the road, or to stock up for your vacation or trip home. Animal-friendly bath and beauty aids and soaps, alternative meat and dairy products, and a small bulk-foods section are all offered. There is also a special emphasis on pet food and care products for our furry friends. Open Mon-Sat 9am-6pm, Sun 12pm-5pm.

YACHATS

Yachats Farmers' Market
Sundays, 9am-2pm, Mid May-Mid October
Yachats Commons (old school on Hwy 101)

Southern Oregon

North Bend
Coos Bay
Coquille
Bandon
42
Roseburg
5
Canyonville
Gold Beach
101
Brookings
Selma
Grants Pass
5
Rogue River
Ashland
Medford
Cascade Range
140
66
Klamath Falls

Maps are for general orientation only
Not drawn to scale
Not all farm towns shown

Southern Oregon

ASHLAND

DINING

Ashland Food Co-op

237 N 1st St • Ashland • (541) 482-2237 • www.ashlandfood.coop

VeryVegFriendly • Deli • Open daily 7am-9pm

If you're hungry, 3 blocks from Ashland's main drag is the Ashland Food Co-op full-service deli, bakery, and juice bar. Indoor and outdoor seating provides the perfect place for breakfast, lunch, or dinner. There are vegan, vegetarian, and omnivore selections. Also features many wheat and/or dairy-free products.

The Breadboard

744 North Main • Ashland • (541) 488-0295

VegFriendly • Sandwiches • Daily breakfast & lunch • Full service • Entrées $5-10

The Breadboard sits on the edge of a drop-off with a great view of the hills across I-5 in the distance. They serve good comfort food. The French toast was amazing. Prices are reasonable.

Dragonfly

241 Hargadine St • Ashland • (541) 488-4855 • www.cantinacollective.com (chef's website)

VegFriendly • Latin/Asian fusion • Daily breakfast, lunch, & dinner • Full service and catering • Entrées $10-20

A California-style restaurant featuring exotic ingredients including plantains and sweet potatoes. The appetizers are delicious. The Big Bowls are all-vegetarian and are full meals in themselves. The menu includes brown rice and organic juices.

Grilla Bites

47 N Main St • Ashland • (541) 488-0889 • www.grillabites.com

VeryVegFriendly • Soup/Sandwich • Mon-Sat, lunch & dinner • Sun lunch Cafeteria • Entrées $5-10

Wonderful salad bar and everything on the menu is either natural or organic. Raw juices are available. Outdoor seating is along the creek behind restaurant. The staff is very friendly and well-informed.

Morning Glory
1149 Siskiyou Blvd • Ashland • (541) 488-8636
www.morninggloryrestaurant.com

VegFriendly • Full breakfasts & light lunches • Full service • Entrées $5-10

The place in Ashland for breakfast. Locals line up before 8am. If you get there after nine, prepare for a long wait. Décor is artsy and whimsical: murals of fairies and rainbows circle the room. Outdoor dining is surrounded by flowers and trees. Food is healthy California-style. Specials are exotic and delicious.

Wiley's World
1606 Ashland St • Ashland • (541) 488-0285 • www.wileysworld.com

VeryVegFriendly • Pastas and salads • Daily lunch and dinner • Full service
Entrées $10-20

Funky décor, casual, and very popular. Pastas are all available without meat, many with tofu options. Pastas are organic, as are most of the salads. Eggless and wheat-free options are available as well. Portions are generous and the staff is friendly.

SHOPPING
Ashland Food Co-op
237 N 1st St • Ashland • (541) 482-2237 • www.ashlandfood.coop

Ashland Community Food Store, located 3 blocks from Ashland's main drag in the heart of the Historic District, has a full-service deli, bakery, and juice bar, along with indoor and outdoor seating to provide the perfect place for breakfast, lunch, or dinner. There are vegan, vegetarian, and omnivore selections. Most notable are the supremely beautiful produce section and the extremely friendly and knowledgeable customer service. Also features many wheat and/or dairy-free products. Open Mon-Sat 8am-9pm, Sun 9am-9pm.

Shop 'n Kart
2268 Ashland St • Ashland • (541) 488-1579

Warehouse-type store featuring organic and conventional products with many deals and deep discounts. Customers bag their own purchases. Open daily 7am-midnight.

FROM THE FARM
Ashland Market-Ashland Armory
Tuesdays, 8:30am-1:30pm, Mid March-Mid November
The National Guard Armory, 1420 East Main Street/Wightman
www.rvgrowersmarket.com

BANDON

Bandon Little Farmers' Market
Saturdays, 10am-2pm or until sold out, July-September
Old Town Bandon, 350 2nd Street

BROOKINGS

Brookings Harbor Farmers' Market
Saturdays, 9am-3pm through Labor Day, Mid June-Mid October
On the Boardwalk -Port of Brookings Harbor, Lower Harbor Rd and Hwy 101

CANYONVILLE

Promise Natural Foods & Bakery
503 S Main St • Canyonville • (541) 839-4167

This country-style natural foods store has bulk foods, a large bulk herb section as well as a full grocery line. The produce is from two certified organic farms in the area. Fresh organic breads and pastries baked Mondays, Wednesdays, and Fridays. Sip organic, free-trade coffee during your visit. Open Mon-Fri 9:30am-6pm, Sat 10am-5pm, Closed Sun.

COOS BAY

Kum Yon's
835 South Broadway • Coos Bay • (541) 269-2662

VegFriendly • Chinese • Daily lunch and dinner • Full service

While the vegetarian menu is small, it will be a welcome treat after a day of sight-seeing on the coast. They serve all the standards: curried vegetables, chow mein, kung pao vegetables, lo mein, stir-fries, etc. All are available with tofu, and brown rice is also available upon request.

Downtown Coos Bay Farmers' Market
Wednesdays, 9am-3pm, Mid May-Mid October
Hwy 101 & Central Ave

COQUILLE

Coquille Farmers' Market
Thursday, 8am-5pm, April-October
Community Center, 1st & Baxter

Southern Oregon

GOLD BEACH

Savory Natural Food Café
29844 Ellensburg Ave • Gold Beach • (541) 247-0297

VeryVegFriendly • Café • Closed Sundays, Closed Saturdays in winter

Very special homemade vegetarian soups, mostly organic sandwiches, salads, and smoothies for indoor seating or take out. Hummus, cranberry chutney, pesto and such are deli items. Muffins baked daily. Home of the "Complete Meal Cookie." An "oasis" with the largest selection of natural and organic foods on the south Oregon coast. Store open 9am Mon-Fri, 11am Sat, closed Sun.

GRANTS PASS

DINING

4th Street Bakery & Deli
200 NW 4th St • Grants Pass • (541) 955-9485

VegFriendly • Breakfast pastries and light lunches • Cafeteria and take out • Entrées under $5 • Closed Sat-Sun

A locally owned bakery where the owner makes everything himself, the 4th Street Bakery & Deli offers fast, friendly service, outdoor tables, and a relaxed, casual atmosphere. There are several bite-sized pastries sold four for a dollar, and the thick soft bread used for their wraps is heavenly. Best pastries in town!

Circle J Café
241 SW G St • Grants Pass • (541) 479-8080

VegFriendly • American • Lunch and dinner • Full service • Entrées $5-10
Closed Sun

A new restaurant, the Circle J Café is the first in the area to offer healthy, natural foods at a great price. The décor is entertainingly eclectic (think 1950's kitsch). The soups are great, the breads are delicious, and the sandwiches come with sweet potato fries. Desserts are worth saving room for and are big enough to share. Beer and wine are available. The restaurant is tiny and very popular; get there early on weekends and be patient.

Sunflower Thai
1571 NE 6th St • Grants Pass • (541) 955-1977

VegFriendly • Thai • Daily lunch and dinner • Full service and take out • Entrées $5-10

While the restaurant's atmosphere is austere, the food selection is wide and tofu can be substituted for meats. Order the "red and black" rice—it's not on the menu—for a real treat with your meal. The restaurant is on the main street into town and has plenty of parking.

SHOPPING

Gooseberries
1533 NE F St • Grants Pass • (541) 471-2700

A small, friendly store with ample parking, Gooseberries carries a wide variety of local organic produce as well as local breads and cheeses. There is a large deli with plenty of vegetarian options. Prices are competitive, and on weekends free samples are demoed. The store carries natural pet foods and a few house and garden plants. The staff is helpful and well-informed. There is a nice selection of frozen foods, including Amy's Kitchen products and soy and rice "ice creams." Open Mon-Sat 8am-8pm, Sun 9:30am-6pm

Sunshine Natural Foods
128 SW H St • Grants Pass • (541) 474-5044

Organic foods, bulk items, health and beauty aids, and a place to sit and eat. The deli has prepared foods, excellent soups, sandwiches, plus a salad and juice bar. They bake many vegan pastries. Award-winning vitamin selection, including food-based vitamins. Open Mon-Fri 9am-6pm, Sat 9am-5pm. Closed Sun.

FROM THE FARM

Grants Pass Growers' Market
Wednesdays, 9am-1pm, June-September
Riverside Park

Saturdays, 9am-1pm, March-November
Corner of F & 4th
www.growersmarket.org

KLAMATH FALLS

Klamath Falls Farmers' Market
Saturdays, 9:30am-1pm, Mid June-Mid October
9th St between Klamath Ave & Main St

MEDFORD

DINING

Kaleidoscope Pizza
3084 Crater Lake Highway • Medford • (541) 779-7787
www.kaleidoscopepizza.com

VeryVegFriendly • Pizza • Daily lunch and dinner • Full service and take out
Entrées $5-10

Kaleidoscope Pizza has a fun and colorful atmosphere, with an emphasis on '60s music and tie-dye décor. The pizzas are excellent and contain a lot of variety. Whole-wheat crust is available, as are large salads and vegetarian soups. The outdoor dining experience is great, with ample shade. Everything is fresh and the staff is friendly.

India Palace
1250 Biddle Road • Medford • (541) 776-3508

VeryVegFriendly • Indian • Mon-Sat lunch and dinner • Full service, buffet, and take out • Entrées $10-20 • Closed Sun

India Palace has a cozy atmosphere—the owner's children often play in a corner or at a booth. The buffet has plenty of vegetarian options, most of them mild enough for people new to Indian cuisine, and can be taken to go. The restaurant is in a popular shopping center.

India's Kitchen
970 N Phoenix Rd #101 • Medford • (541) 773-6800

VeryVegFriendly • Indian • Daily lunch and dinner • Full service, buffet, and take out • Entrées $5-10

The food is the most authentic Indian cooking to be found in southern Oregon, but the chef will spice dishes mildly unless asked to do otherwise. The variety is very good, and the ambiance is great (the restaurant is formal enough for special occasions). The Thali dinner is a sampling treat. The location is easy to find and there is plenty of parking.

Thai Bistro
535 Stevens St • Medford • (541) 772-6200

VeryVegFriendly • Thai • Mon–Sat. lunch and dinner • Full service, buffet, and take out • Entrées $5-10 • Closed Sun

The great décor of Thai Bistro includes a saltwater fish tank. While vegetarian choices at the buffet can be limited, the service is attentive and lunchtime can be very popular.

SHOPPING

Adventist Book Center & Veg Foods
632 Crater Lake Ave • Medford • (541) 734-0567

Very popular with the vegetarian community. A large selection of vegetarian foods, including a very wide selection of vegetarian meat replacement foods such as analogs for chili, hot dogs, burgers, etc. Organic foods, bulk products, healthy snack foods, soy milks, soups, etc. Books on health and nutrition and cookbooks. Open Mon-Thurs 11am-6pm, Sun 11am-3pm. Closed Fri-Sat.

FROM THE FARM

Medford Growers' & Crafters' Market
Thursdays, 8:30am-1:30pm, Mid March-Mid November
The Medford Armory, 1701 South Pacific Hwy & Stewart
www.rvgrowersmarket.com

NORTH BEND

SHOPPING

Bailey's Health Food Center
2235 Newmark • North Bend • (541) 756-3004

With a little bit of everything, Bailey's Health Food Center can help you stock your vacation getaway kitchen or resupply your picnic basket for the family car trip. Recharge yourself at the juice bar with one of their freshly made, classic combinations or make up your own favorite. Open Mon-Sat 9am-6:30pm, Sun 10am-5:30pm.

Coos Head Food Store
1960 Sherman Ave • North Bend • (541) 756-7264

A small store but with the selection and variety usually only found in larger stores. Vegetarians will find all or most of what they need in this store including meat analogues, tempeh and tofu, and an excellent organic produce section. They also stock a good variety of herbs, supplements, and animal-free health and beauty aids. The staff is especially helpful. This is an important resource for the southern Oregon coastal communities.

ROSEBURG

DINING

Taco Del Mar
368 NE Winchester • Roseburg • (541) 440-5206 • www.tacodelmar.com
See review – Beaverton

SHOPPING

New Day Quality Grocery
210 SE Jackson St • Roseburg • (541) 672-0275

A 100% meat-free store carrying fresh organic produce, organic foods, bulk items, and non-food items including books, clothing, kitchenware, health information, nutrition center, and beauty aids. Open Mon-Fri 9:30am-6:30pm, Sat 9:30am-5:30pm. Closed Sun.

Southern Oregon

153

FROM THE FARM

Umpqua Valley Farmers' Market
Saturdays, 9am-1pm, Mid April-October
2400 Stewart Parkway

SELMA

Selma Farmers' Market
Sundays, 9am-1pm, June-September
Selma Community Center, 18255 Hwy 199

Vegetarians of Washington

Something special is happening in the state of Washington. A new kind vegetarian society, Vegetarians of Washington, is growing by leaps and bounds and now has a membership numbering in the thousands. Vegetarians of Washington, an independent 501(c)3 non-profit organization founded in 2001, is already one of the largest and most dynamic regional vegetarian society in the United States and has the most enthusiastic and devoted members and supporters anywhere.

What makes Vegetarians of Washington so different? First is our membership. Vegetarians of Washington is made up of people from all walks of life. You don't even have to be a vegetarian to join! We don't ask and we don't tell. We welcome everyone whether they're an experienced vegetarian, a beginner or just curious.

Second is our approach. Vegetarians of Washington follows the education and advocacy model. We teach, we encourage, and we try to have as much fun as we can while we do it. We're not activists. We don't hit people over the head with the tofu. Instead, we believe in providing a "can do" atmosphere where everyone proceeds at their own pace and just does the best they can as they change over to a vegetarian diet.

Third are our events. We enjoy great-tasting food and will accept nothing less. We hold gourmet monthly dining events at the Mount Baker Club in Seattle, where you can enjoy a delicious multi-course meal from a different local restaurant, chef, or cookbook author each month, and you can also meet lots of interesting people at one convenient location. We also hold free, informative nutrition and cooking classes at locations throughout western Washington.

Our biggest event, Vegfest, held in March of each year in Seattle, Washington, is the largest vegetarian food festival in the United States. Vegfest features over 600 different kinds of food to try, talks on health and nutrition by doctors and dieticians, cooking demonstrations by chefs and cookbook authors, a huge vegetarian bookstore, and a special children's program. Vegfest is attended by thousands of people and is staffed by over 700 volunteers who serve over 500,000 samples of food each year.

Fourth are our benefits. Our members receive a free subscription to the popular *Vegetarian Times* magazine. This unique magazine is packed full of both vegetarian and vegan recipes and the latest nutritional information. Our discount program entitles members to discounts at local restaurants and a wide range of businesses. Members also receive a reduced price at our dinners and special members' appreciation events.

Fifth are our books. *Vegetarian Pacific Northwest* is the latest book project of the Vegetarians of Washington, and the organization has devoted considerable time and effort to its production. We have written three books prior to this. The first was a guidebook to vegetarian dining, shopping and living in Washington and Oregon, called *Veg-Feasting in the Pacific Northwest*. This book was used as a starting point for *Vegetarian Pacific Northwest*. The second is *The Veg-Feasting Cookbook* where we invited many local veg-friendly restaurants and chefs to share their very best recipes. Third is **The Vegetarian Solution**, written by vice president Stewart Rose, giving up-to-date information on how a vegetarian diet can improve your health and the world in which you live. Our books are currently available in fine bookstores everywhere or online.

Sixth is our work with vegetarian and veg-friendly businesses. Manufacturers, distributors, and retailers of vegetarian foods and vegetarian restaurants form the vital links in our food chain. We work in many capacities to support those who bring us the food we eat thus closing the circle between producers and consumers.

Many wonderful people have joined Vegetarians of Washington. We meet their needs by creating a positive atmosphere where they can socialize, have fun, eat great food together, and reinforce their excellent choice to follow a vegetarian diet. Please join us! For more information, please visit us on the Web at www.VegOfWA.org or give us a call at (206) 706-2635. To join, visit www.VegOfWA.org/joinus.html

Index of Towns

Lake Forest Park, WA 34
Lake Oswego, OR 105
Lakewood, WA 34
Langley, WA 15
La Grande, OR 106
Leavenworth, WA 87
Lincoln City, OR 140
Longview, WA 66
Lorane, OR 141
Lynnwood, WA 34
Madras, OR 141
Manzanita, OR 106
Maple Falls, WA 15
Marysville, WA 15
McMinnville, OR 106
Medford, OR 151
Mill Creek, WA 35
Milwaukie, OR 107
Millwood, WA 87
Monroe, WA 35
Morton, WA 67
Moses Lake, WA 87
Mount Lake Terrace, WA 35
Mount Vernon, WA 15
Mukilteo, WA 36
Napavine, WA 67
Newport, OR 141
Newport, WA 87
North Bend, OR 153
North Bend, WA 36
North Plains, OR 107
Noti, OR 142
Oak Harbor, WA 16
Okanogan, WA 88
Olga, WA 16
Olympia, WA 67
Omak, WA 88
Oregon City, OR 108
Othello, WA 88
Pasco, WA 88
Pendleton, OR 108
Philomath, OR 142
Port Angeles, WA 74
Port Orchard, WA 75
Port Townsend, WA 76

Portland, OR 108
Poulsbo, WA 78
Prineville, OR 142
Prosser, WA 88
Pullman, WA 88
Puyallup, WA 36
Quilcene, WA 79
Rainier, OR 124
Raymond, WA 69
Redmond, OR 142
Redmond, WA 37
Renton, WA 38
Republic, WA 89
Richland, WA 89
Rickreall, OR 143
Rochester, WA 69
Roseburg, OR 153
Roslyn, WA 90
Salem, OR 143
Sammamish, WA 39
Scappoose, OR 124
Seaside, OR 124
Seatac, WA 39
Seattle, WA 40
Sedro Woolley, WA 17
Selma, OR 154
Sequim, WA 79
Shelton, WA 79
Sherwood, OR 125
Shoreline, WA 56
Silverdale, WA 79
Silverton, OR 144
Snohomish, WA 56
Snoqualmie, WA 56
Spokane, WA 90
Sumner, WA 57
Tacoma, WA 57
Tenino, WA 69
Tigard, OR 125
Tillamook, OR 125
Tonasket, WA 92
Troutdale, OR 126
Tualatin, OR 126
Tukwila, WA 59
Tumwater, WA 69

BOOK PUBLISHING COMPANY

since 1974—books that educate, inspire, and empower

To find your favorite vegetarian and soyfood products online,
visit: www.healthy-eating.com

Tofu Cookery
25th Anniversary Edition
Louise Hagler
978-1-57067-220-0 $18.95

More Fabulous Beans
Barb Bloomfield
978-1-57067-146-3 $14.95

Soup's On
Barb Bloomfield
978-1-57067-047-3 $10.95

More Books from Vegetarians of Washington

Meatless Burgers
Louise Hagler
978-1-57067-087-9 $9.95

The Veg-Feasting Cookbook
Vegetarians of Washington
978-1-57067-178-4 $18.95

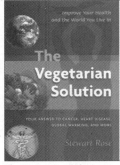

The Vegetarian Solution
Stewart Rose
978-1-57067-205-7 $12.95

Purchase these health titles and cookbooks from your local bookstore or
natural food store, or you can buy them directly from:

Book Publishing Company • P.O. Box 99 • Summertown, TN 38483
1-800-695-2241

Please include $3.95 per book for shipping and handling.